POLICE PSYCHOLOGY

POLICE PSYCHOLOGY

A New Specialty and New Challenges for Men and Women in Blue

David J. Thomas

Forensic Psychology
David J. Thomas, Series Editor

AN IMPRINT OF ABC-CLIO, LLC
Santa Barbara, California • Denver, Colorado • Oxford, England

Library of Congress Cataloging-in-Publication Data

Thomas, David J.
  Police psychology : a new specialty and new challenges for men and women in blue /
David J. Thomas.
     p. cm. — (Forensic psychology)
  Includes bibliographical references and index.
  ISBN 978-0-313-38728-9 (hard copy : alk. paper) — ISBN 978-0-313-38729-6 (ebook)
1. Police psychology.   2. Police—Job stress.   3. Criminal psychology.   I. Title.
  HV7936.P75.T46   2011
  363.201'9—dc22   2011002674

ISBN: 978-0-313-38728-9
EISBN: 978-0-313-38729-6

15 14 13 12 11   1 2 3 4 5

This book is also available on the World Wide Web as an eBook.
Visit www.abc-clio.com for details.

Praeger
An Imprint of ABC-CLIO, LLC

ABC-CLIO, LLC
130 Cremona Drive, P.O. Box 1911
Santa Barbara, California 93116-1911

This book is printed on acid-free paper ∞

Manufactured in the United States of America

This text is dedicated to:
Patricia, Jermaine, Raevyn, Erika, and Champ

Contents

The History and Application of Police Psychology

INTRODUCTION

When one thinks of police and police psychology, one might assume that the practice of police psychology has been around almost as long as the profession, which dates back some 200 years, but police psychology is a relatively new specialty, which falls under the umbrella of forensic psychology. Although the profession of policing dates back to the early 1800s, it wasn't until 1908 that it began developing standards and training for police recruits. The first such professional training program was established by August Vollmer in Berkeley, California. Vollmer (1936) is considered the father of modern American policing, and he advocated written tests, intelligence testing, oral boards, physical fitness testing, neurological tests—all of the aforementioned information to be passed onto a psychiatrist to evaluate the candidate's fitness for duty—and finally a background investigation (pp. 228–231).

Today, many of the innovations prescribed by Vollmer have been adopted by most agencies, based in part or in whole on the needs of the organization. The science of police psychology is relatively new, and this chapter establishes its humble beginnings and then provides a road map for the remainder of the text.

A BRIEF HISTORY OF POLICE PSYCHOLOGY

The first intelligence test for police selection was administered by Terman et al. (1917) for the San Jose Police Department. The test was administered as an experiment; however, Terman et al. noted that there needed to be future research, especially the correlation of scores from psychological tests to the success of the candidates. They also noted that in order for such tests to be valuable, norms had to be established with cutoffs (p. 29).

Law enforcement agencies were slow in accepting these standards primarily due to the political nature of policing, which dates back to a period in time that preceded Vollmer and was the impetus for his demands. Even today, many law enforcement administrators do not require a psychological assessment of new hires. As one chief of a midsize police department stated when questioned regarding his hiring process: "I know people; after I review their hiring packet and personally interview them, I can tell you if they have a psychological problem. All the damn psychologist is going to do is administer a test, score it, and tell me if the person is a suitable candidate, all for $200, and that's money I can use for something else."

The aforementioned statement is reflective of a much deeper sentiment within the profession of policing, which is the lack of trust in the mental health profession. As you will discover, there exists an uneasy peace between police and the field of psychology, an uneasiness that will be explored in the first half of this text. Simply put, the profession of policing is a closed subculture, and police are not very trusting of outsiders. The police psychologist is perceived as having a great deal of power over police officers because the psychologist can determine if a candidate is suitable for hire; may be asked to counsel an officer after a critical incident; may be asked to complete a fit-for-duty assessment; and can ultimately make the determination that an officer is no longer suitable for duty, which can result in a recommendation of termination.

From a historical perspective, Scrivner and Kurke (1995) explain that there have been three evolving eras or traditions that define the field of police psychology:

1. The first period was established with the passing of the Crime Control Bill of 1968, which established the Law Enforcement Assistance Administration (LEAA), an agency that is no longer in existence. Much of the research performed by psychologists during the LEAA era was associated in the development of selection standards (p. 4).

2. The second phase can be described as direct delivery of psychological services to police personnel (p. 5). Interestingly, this phase is the one most prevalent today. Although the first experiment relative to testing police candidates dates back to 1916, the first in-house police psychologist was hired by the Los Angeles Police Department in 1968 (Reiser, 1970). Today, agencies may contract part-time mental health services with an outside mental health provider or they may hire a full-time in-house person. The problem here is that there is no universal

standard for the delivery of services, and it could be as simple as testing for pre-employment or as complex as providing services to police after a critical incident. In any instance, the agency defines what services it wants and needs.

3. The third phase is widely used today as well and includes career development and the application of psychological principles to such areas as criminal profiling, hostage negotiations, and eyewitness identification, which will be addressed in great detail in the second half of this text. Here again, the application of psychology to police practices has become an accepted practice, dating back to the 1950s when psychiatrist James Brussel distinguished himself as the first criminal profiler by developing a profile of the suspect known as the Mad Bomber in New York City (Brussel, 1968).

DEFINING POLICE PSYCHOLOGY

As noted earlier, police psychology is considered a subspecialty of forensic psychology, and as of this writing, there is a movement to make it a specialty. That movement has been spearheaded by three organizations: Division 18 of the American Psychological Association, the Psychologists in Public Service; the International Association of Chiefs of Police: Police Psychological Services Sections (IACP-PPSS); and the Society for Police and Criminal Psychology. Unlike the traditional specialties in the field of psychology, there really is no specialized training or clinical rotation for police psychology. Most of those who practice in the field have a profound interest in the law enforcement profession. A simple definition of police psychology is the application of the principles of psychology to law enforcement (Bartol & Bartol, 2008; Reiser, 1970) (see Diagram 1-1: The Specialty of Police Psychology).

CONCLUSION

The remainder of this text is devoted to offering insight into many of the topics detailed in Diagram 1-1, which outlines the specialties and applications of police psychology. It is important to understand the development of the police personality and how the job impacts officers' perceptions and actions when it comes to interacting in both their professional and personal lives.

Psychologists are clear that officers come from diverse backgrounds, and there is no such thing as the ideal police personality (Kenney & Watson, 1999; Bartol & Bartol, 2008). The police personality is shaped through a series of common experiences, which begin with academy training. Through those experiences, officers develop skepticism, cynicism, and suspiciousness and create a persona of distance that is used as a barrier/shield to protect their being and humanity from as much trauma and psychological damage as they possibly can. As you read each chapter, never lose focus of chapter 2

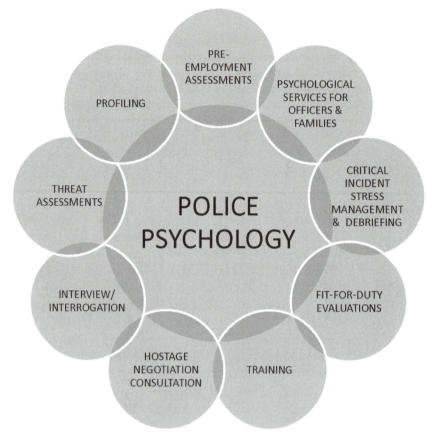

Diagram 1-1: The Specialty of Police Psychology

and the discussion of the police personality and how that personality impacts every aspect of policing. Then reflect on these two questions: How would the things I see each day impact my life professionally and personally? And would those experiences change or destroy my life as I know it?

REFERENCES

Bartol, C. R., & Bartol, A. M. (2008). *Introduction to forensic psychology: Research and application* (2nd ed.). Thousand Oaks, CA: Sage Publications.

Brussel, J. (1968). *Casebook of a crime psychiatrist.* New York: Bernard Gies Associates.

Kenney, D. J., & Watson, T. S. (1999). Intelligence and the selection of the police recruit. In D. J. Kenney & R. P. McNamara (Eds.), *Police and policing* (2nd ed., pp. 15–36). Westport, CT: Greenwood Publishing.

McKenzie, J. D. (1984). Preface. In J. T. Reese & H. A. Goldstein (Eds.), *Federal Bureau of Investigation Symposium. Psychological services for law enforcement (Preface)*. Washington, DC: Federal Bureau of Investigation.

Reiser, M. (1970). *The police department psychologist.* Springfield, IL: Charles C. Thomas.

Scrivner, E. M. & Kurke, M. I. (1995). Police psychology at the dawn of the 21st century. In M. I. Kurke & E. M. Scrivner (Eds.), *Police psychology into the 21st century* (pp. 3–30). Hillsdale, NJ: Lawrence Erlbaum Associates.

Terman, L. M., Otis, A. S., Dickson, V., Hubbard, A. S., Norton, J. K., & Howard, L., et al. (1917). A trial of mental and pedagogical tests in a civil service examination for policemen and firemen. *Journal of Applied Psychology, 1,* 17–29.

Vollmer, A. (1936). *The police and modern society.* Berkeley, CA: Regents of the University of California.

The Police Personality

INTRODUCTION

The police personality is an enigma. Some researchers argue that it is unique to the police subculture, while others argue the police personality is a direct result of the socialization process. Still others argue that there is no such thing as a police personality. As someone who has spent 20 years in the profession and 30 years teaching in the academy, I still wonder if there is a distinct personality. Adlam (1981) argues after reviewing the literature that there is no clear answer, and the literature is contradictory at best (p. 153).

This chapter will allow you to view police actions, summaries of investigations into acts of brutality and perceived bias, and the impact that race has on an officer's perception, and it will provide you with insight into what can be characterized as the police personality. However, before delving further into this chapter, the two hypotheses that attempt to explain the police personality will be examined. Based on your prior knowledge of policing and what you believe the police personality to be, choose one of the hypotheses. At the end of the chapter, you can determine if your selection is correct. More importantly, reflect on how you made the selection and what, if anything, changed your opinion.

Hypothesis 1: The police personality is a myth because police officers come from many backgrounds with varying educational levels, life experiences, and socioeconomic status. Yet what make the personality unique are the officers' shared experiences.

Hypothesis 2: The police personality is very real, and agencies look for a particular type of candidate. The personality traits an agency seeks are authoritative, suspicious, honorable, loyal, secretive, individualistic, and conservative, as with these traits the perfect officer can be created through the socialization process.

WHY WOULD ANYONE WANT TO BE A POLICE OFFICER?

For the past 30 years, I have asked the aforementioned question, and more often than not, I am told by police recruits and university students that they want to help people. I have often pondered their response, wondering if they really understand the profession of policing. In my mind are visions of dead bodies, verbal abuse by victims and suspects, demands and threats by the public, and at times, being spit on or physically assaulted. Another common answer is: "It is a good job with benefits and where I don't have to worry about layoffs." This second group is usually older, understanding the importance of job security and a pension. However, what's missing is passion for the job; their response can be interpreted as nonempathetic, viewing the position as just a job. A third group offers that they want to be police officers because of the excitement, believing it is just like what they see on television. To me, this group is the most dangerous because they fail to realize their role in society, a failure that can cause irreparable damage to the profession (Thomas, 2011).

Policing is unique in that it is challenging, and in many cases, new officers enter a world that Herman (1997) describes as man's inhumanity to man. If we just look at the concept of helping others, then we are dealing with the victims of crime and their families. Although tragic when thinking of a murdered child or loved one, there is satisfaction in bringing a suspect to justice. Reflect on the concept of helping citizens, and the challenge in such cases is remaining objective. Below are five incidents—each was a request for assistance. After reviewing each incident, examine the paradox between help and the final outcome.

- During an arrest for domestic violence, the wife turns on the officers and attacks them, stating that she loves her husband. She has been beaten so badly that one eye is swollen shut and she has broken ribs.
- A prostitute is beaten with a hanger by her pimp. The beating is so severe that she is hospitalized for weeks, yet during the interview by police, she states: "I deserved the beating; I didn't make any money." The victim refuses to press charges.

- An officer recovers a stolen moped for an elderly citizen. The next day, the same officer responds to a fatal accident where the elderly man was killed riding the moped that the officer recovered.
- An officer responds with lights and siren to a robbery and shooting. The officer enters an intersection on the way to that crime site and hits an innocent bystander's car, killing the occupants.
- Officers respond to a family's request to assist their son, who has a history of paranoid schizophrenia. After police arrive, the son experiences a psychotic episode and attacks officers so violently that they have no choice but to shoot and kill the son to stop the attack.

If we examine the aforementioned incidents, no matter the reason for becoming a police officer, they have an impact on an officer's view of the world and, more importantly, the community in which an officer serves. To really understand the police personality, we must begin with the socialization process. Keep in mind that as human beings, we may all possess certain personality traits, including sensitivity, flexibility, curiosity, trust, risk taking, a willingness to help, concern for others, survival, and cognitive processing (Meggitt, 2006; Newman & Newman, 2008). Do you believe that any of these traits are essential in policing?

THE SOCIALIZATION PROCESS

The socialization process may begin prior to entering the academy with a new candidate attempting to think like a cop and placing themselves in the position of an officer when it comes to decision making. A future officer may read every book, watch every television show, and see every movie/video available in an attempt to understand policing. However, what is missing from this equation is an understanding that each community has different needs and places different demands on its police department. Some of the variables that impact an agency and the officer are the style of policing adopted by the agency, the agency size, and the police organization. In essence, the resources available to a candidate may offer very little insight into the reality of policing. Instead, there is often some symbol that makes the profession attractive to the candidate: a relative in policing, power and excitement, becoming or knowing a victim of crime, or contact with the local police.

The police academy is where the socialization process begins. With that said, there are many versions of the police academy in the United States. Law enforcement training is mandated by state statues where the oversight is given to state training commissions or Police Officer Standards and Training (POST) Councils, which provide training for some 17,876 law enforcement agencies within the United States (U.S. Department of Justice, 2007). Since there is no universal standard, the number of training hours and the type of academy varies by state. For instance, some states require that all of their police trainees attend one state facility for training, while other states have regional training academies, and others hire and train their own officers. As you envision the socialization process and the beginning of an officer's career, examine these three academy styles. Which would you rather attend—a state academy, a regional academy, or an agency-run academy?

1. The **state academies** usually require trainees to spend the night and give them the weekends off. It is total immersion into the police process requiring trainees to eat, sleep, and drink policing, much like attending military basic training. State training facilities are staffed by state law enforcement personnel or full-time training staff not affiliated with any one department.
2. **Regional academies** usually allow trainees to go home at the end of each day. They are staffed by officers from local agencies and supplemented by a cadre of officers working part time. There are two kinds of trainees attending regional academies: those who are paying their way to attend and hope to get a job upon graduation, and those who are agency sponsored.
3. **Agency-run academies** hire and train their officers. At the local level, trainees go home at the end of the day. However, the trainee is indoctrinated with training goals that meet the state standard, but more importantly, they learn the expectations of the organization.

If we are to rank the academies in order of impact on a new officer's psyche, we have to begin with the state academies as having the most impact, especially those that train their own officers, such as the 49 state police/trooper academies in the United States (U.S. Department of Justice, 2007). The only state that does not have a state police academy is Hawaii, because it has no state police organization.

Second in terms of impact are the agency-run academies because they prepare an officer from day one for a specific organization, and in that role, the trainee learns what it is to be an officer of the Anywhere Police Department. The difference between this setting and the state academy is that the trainees are allowed to go home at the end of each day.

Last in the pecking order are the regional academies. Regional academies take on many different formats, the most common being those run by community colleges and/or universities. Because of the setting, some regional academies integrate traditional college courses where the trainee obtains a two-year degree as well as police certification. Others offer the training independent of the traditional college setting and grant college credit upon completion of the academy.

In the regional setting, many of the trainees pay their own way and upon graduation can apply to any police agency. Also, this group of trainees is allowed to go home each day, and because they are not associated with an agency, they have no reason to become socialized. In fact, this group is at a disadvantage because when they are hired they have to change their focus from the basic skill set taught in the academy to becoming socialized and meeting agency expectations. Agencies recognize the benefit of running their own academy, yet they realize the economic benefit of not having to pay salary and benefits for a trainee who has already completed training (Dempsey & Frost, 2010; Siegel, 2010).

THE FIELD-TRAINING OFFICER (FTO) PROGRAM

The FTO program is where a new candidate begins after having successfully graduated from the police academy. The FTO program is usually 16 weeks of training where the theory and scenarios that candidates were exposed to in the academy are applied to real-world events. In essence, it is on-the-job training where the rubber meets the road. The trainee is evaluated in four core areas: performance, knowledge, attitude, and appearance, with each of these areas having a number of criteria. The ultimate goal is to create a product that meets organizational needs and the demands of the community. This is also where both the agency and the new officer determine if they are compatible during a one-year probationary period. The challenges a new candidate may face are as follows:

- The trainee does not view the world as their peers do.
- The value system of the trainee may be in conflict with the values of the organization.
- There may be limited opportunity for promotion.

In policing, as within any organization, there must be compatibility with ethics and values in order for the system to work (Dion, 1994). If such conflicts arise and a trainee is not compatible, they usually wash out of the FTO program or resign after the first year to find an agency that is compatible with them professionally as well as personally. At the very core of this conflict may be such issues as unwritten policies, which oftentimes are in conflict with state law or agency written directives (see Scenario 2-1).

SCENARIO 2-1 TRAFFIC STOPS A MATTER OF BLACK AND WHITE

You are a trainee in the FTO program. Your training officer has been careful to expose you to the diversity of the community, wanting you to understand its many facets. However, you notice a trend when it comes to working in the black community, and it is not just with your training officer but with every white officer who works in the black community. The agency policy provides discretion when it comes to making traffic stops, and in your state, it is illegal to mandate a quota when it comes to writing citations. However, the unwritten policy is to stop every black male on a bicycle who violates traffic statutes or rides his bicycle at night without a light because in most cases they have arrest warrants, act as look outs for drug dealers on the corner, or are in possession of drugs/drug paraphernalia. Yet white cyclists travel the streets of the city committing the same violations and are never stopped, let alone ticketed. It could be argued that the traffic violations by black cyclists were committed, so officers can make the stops and write the citations, but the practice is biased.

As a trainee, you ask your training officer: Why is there a different standard? He replies: "This is just the way it is. You know in the short time you have been here where all the violent crime occurs, who has the weapons, and who the suspects are—and it sure isn't the white cyclist. This is our way of preventing crime before it gets started. If we catch them now before a crime is committed, then we have done our job serving and protecting our community. Let me tell you something, if you want to be a success here, then this is your job, or else you won't fit in."

Reflective Questions

1.   As a new officer, what are your personal views regarding such a practice? The issue of racial profiling has been an issue in every state. In the state of Florida, it was such an issue that an in-service training program was developed around the issue of diversity and discriminatory traffic stops, entitled *Discriminatory Profiling and Professional Traffic Stops.*

2.   Do you believe that the administration is aware of such practices? Yes. Such actions may not be known by the CEO of the organization, but they are known by first-line supervisors up to and including shift commanders.

3. Why do administrators allow this to happen? Policing is a business just like any other profession. How does an agency prove to a community that it is having an impact on crime? Through the use of crime statistics. From an administrative standpoint, the greater the numbers produced—be they arrests or citations—and whether those numbers can be correlated to a reduction in crime equates to community support.

4. Can and do such actions have an adverse impact on certain aspects of a community? Yes. Despite the efforts of community policing, such acts create an us-versus-them mentality. Now think of the new officer attempting to fit in; the message is participate or find a new job.

5. In discussing justice and equity, do these acts defy logic? Yes. It shows that police can be biased and that in some cases an entire agency can be biased toward one aspect of the community. There is a historical root of this bias that dates back to the days of slavery and the slave patrols of the 1800s.

6. Is this an issue of compatibility? It depends on the new officer's value system. If he or she loves the agency, this may be where they belong. On the other hand, the officer may hate the organizational culture and determine after the first year that it is time to move to another agency.

A BRIEF HISTORY OF BIAS IN POLICING

In minority communities, police are often seen as an occupying army. This is not without some historical basis. In the 1700s and 1800s, one of the many duties the U.S. Marshal Service was charged with included returning runaway slaves, and in the 1800s, Southern sheriffs routinely supervised slave patrols (Hadden, 2001). Police bias has continued since that time, as evidenced by the following investigations:

- 1930—The Wickersham Commission investigated what is best described as lawlessness in law enforcement (Walker & Boehm, 1997).
- 1967—The Kerner Commission of 1967 investigated the cause of the violent riots in Detroit and Newark, noting the poor relationship between blacks and police (Kerner Commission, 1968).
- 1970—The Knapp Commission investigated the New York City Police Department and corruption within the ranks (Knapp Commission, 1972).
- 1976—The U.S. Senate investigation of the FBI Counterintelligence Program looked into the FBI's covert action programs against U.S. citizens and

its efforts to discredit visionaries like Dr. Martin Luther King Jr. (Churchill & Vander Wall, 2002).

- 1991—The Christopher Commission investigation of the Los Angeles Police Department after the Rodney King incident determined that the agency had a poor relationship with minority communities along with a number of other issues (City of Los Angeles, 1991).
- 1992—The Mollen Commission was charged with investigating the New York City Police Department regarding charges of corruption. The commission also determined that acts of brutality were common in large drug-infested minority communities (City of New York, 1994).
- 2000—The Rampart Independent Review Committee was charged with investigating the Los Angeles Police Department's Rampart Division and a scandal known as the Rampart scandal. Central to its findings were issues of brutality and misconduct (Rampart Independent Review Panel, 2000).

When evaluating the commissions that were impaneled to investigate police behavior and poor relationships with minority communities, as a reader you may wonder why the police haven't changed as societal attitudes toward minorities have improved. Could it be that what agencies select as the perfect personality for policing actually contributes to racism? Or can officers be screened to determine who will display this behavior?

CAMARADERIE OF THE BADGE

As an institution, policing has been noted for being a tight group or a closed subculture. It involves a unique perspective of life and humanity because the police always see the worst in their fellow human beings. The end result is that as a culture, the police shut the rest of the world out and simply state: "No one will understand this except another cop." This one phrase is akin to groupthink where a group develops cohesiveness through similar experiences and there are expectations of conformity, which allows each member to view the world through the same set of lenses (Janis, 1972). Yet the research into police behavior and culture is conflicting at times.

In a 1996 study of the New York City Police Department conducted by Amnesty International, it was determined that the number of complaints received against officers was in direct proportion to the racial composition of the New York City Police Department (p. 11). The results of this study suggest that policing is more about culture than race.

However ,Wisebud, Greenspan, Hamilton, Williams, and Bryant (2000) conducted a survey of 900 police officers in Illinois and Ohio regarding their attitudes toward police brutality with some interesting results, most notably, that the race of an officer defines how he/she perceives the delivery of police service and contact between police and citizens. In their research, Wisebud et al. were very specific about asking questions that were neutral from an officer's perspective, meaning that the questions were not dependent on an officer's race but rather on her view of police practices. Although the Amnesty International (1996) research would lead one to believe that race has little to do with police practices, Wisebud et al. makes it clear that race is central to an officer's perspective.

The first such contradiction can be found in officers' perceptions about the use of excessive force. White officers believe on average that race is rarely (between 5% and 12% of the time) a determining factor in the use of force or the use of excessive force (Wisebud et al., 2000, p. 9). However, 74 percent of the respondent minority officers perceive race and socioeconomic status as a determining factor in how minority citizens are treated when compared to the treatment of their white counterparts in similar situations (Wisebud et al., 2000, p. 9). How could there be such a disparity? What is so different? Is there a historical context by which minority officers view contact between police and citizens? Go back and examine scenario 2-1; it is more common than one would like to think. What are the practices of the veteran officers? Therein lies the answer to the disparity: perception is the individual's reality.

Thomas (2000) investigated officer's perceptions and observations of race in an unpublished study of 100 officers in the southeastern United States. The demographics of the officers were as follows: 80 were white males, 10 were black males, and 10 were white females averaging 10 years of service and representing 10 different agencies.

- One hundred percent (N = 100) of the officers were aware of acts of discrimination by their fellow officers.
- Ninety percent (N = 80 white males, N = 5 white females, and N = 5 black males) responded that the administration was aware of the situation and nothing had been done in any of the cases, not even corrective counseling by the first-line supervisors.
- Eighty percent (N = 54 white males, N = 2 white females, and N = 8 black males) noted that racial slurs were the most common form of discriminatory acts.
- Eighty percent (N = 8 black males) noted the use of racial slurs and went on to describe acts of excessive force that they had witnessed. None of the white officers, male or female, were aware of any incidents of excessive force or brutality. The black officers observed the behavior but did not report the violations; they noted that it was easier to intervene or stop the acts than to report the white officers involved for fear that they would be ostracized. This is contrary to the study by Wisebud et al. (2000).
- Sixty-five percent (N = 59 white males) noted their agency had participated in discriminatory assignments within the agency, stating that preference had

been given to females and blacks in such assignments as community policing, personnel, detectives, and promotions. In contrast, 80 percent of the white females ($N = 8$) and black males ($N = 8$) did not perceive this as a problem.

Wisebud et al. and Thomas offer some insights into the code of silence among officers, which is central to officer misconduct. The respondents to both surveys agreed that if they were to turn in a fellow officer, they would receive the cold shoulder from fellow officers. Moreover, they reported looking the other way when an officer was involved in acts of misconduct in excess of 50 percent of the time (Wisebud et al., 2000, p. 5). The code of silence is an obstruction to justice and provides protection for those who commit acts of misconduct; it has as its foundation loyalty (Abel, 2006; Skolnick, 2005). To snitch on another officer may be career suicide, or worse yet, it could mean that backup is slow to arrive when assistance is needed. Examine the following incidents. Do they support your chosen hypothesis?

Four Incidents of Police Brutality

- 1992—Black motorist Malice Green was beaten to death by members of the Detroit Police Department. Three white officers participated in the beating while a black sergeant stood by failing to intervene. Two of the officers involved in the beating were sentenced to a term of 7 to 15 years (Sigelman, Welch, Bledsoe, & Combs, 1997).
- 1997—Haitian immigrant Abner Louima was arrested and sexually assaulted when a New York City police officer dragged Louima from his cell and took a broken wooden plunger handle and rammed it in Louima's anus. The officer was white and was sentenced to 30 years in prison (Kocieniewski, 1997).
- 1999—Amadou Diallo, a West African immigrant, was shot and killed by four New York City police officers. The officers fired 41 rounds at Diallo when they thought he was reaching for a gun but was actually reaching for his wallet. The four officers were acquitted (Fritsch, 2000).
- 2006—Sean Bell was shot and killed by New York City police officers after striking a police undercover van. Bell's vehicle was fired upon 50 times with 21 rounds striking his vehicle. Bell's car was occupied by two other black males, and none of the three were armed. There were three officers involved in the Bell shooting, two were black and one was white, and all were acquitted of any crime (McFadden, 2006).

The aforementioned incidents were selected at random without examining the race of the officers. In fact, they were selected because of their notoriety. If we examine the media responses to each incident, they were portrayed as a matter of race—white versus black. Yet the officers who participated were black and white.

In evaluating the research, it is clear that the perception of officers is determined by race. However, there appear to be two intangibles that cross all boundaries: the camaraderie of the badge and peer pressure. The concept of misconduct or bias, however, is due to much more than peer pressure and/or camaraderie. In order for such behavior to flourish, there must be a permissive atmosphere where officers feel comfortable that they will not be disciplined for their actions. Most troubling in this equation is that officers are taught ethics in the academy and are held to a standard where ethical conduct is the norm. In addition to the ethical standards of the academy, trainees are taught the importance of the cohesiveness of the badge and coming together as a unit in order to survive on the street. Officers who find themselves in this quandary have as a supporting cast their oath of office, duty to citizens, and responsibility to their family.

Competing against the oath, duty, and family are the friendships that have been forged in the academy/within the agency, surviving life-threatening events together, loyalty, and security (See Diagram 2-1). When examined in this light, doing what is ethical becomes much more difficult for some and

Diagram 2-1: Camaraderie of the Badge

can challenge one's belief system. Failure to support the efforts of the group could well mean that an officer is ousted by the very group they covet. Trompetter (1984) argues that the solidarity of the squad room leads to solitary solidarity, which when examined closely means that the camaraderie of the badge comes before all else, groupthink. Trompetter also notes that this solidarity can destroy a marriage, replace individuality with that of a group identity, and foster alcoholism as well as poor physical health (p. 535).

THE POLICE PERSONALITY

Reiser (1972) states that there is no such thing as a police personality, noting that those who enter policing come from a variety of backgrounds (p. 81). If we work from the hypothesis that there is no such thing as a police personality, then why are officers so similar in their thinking and behavior? If we think of a new officer who learns to steady themselves during the field-training program, and if we reexamine the five incidents introduced at the beginning of this chapter, we can begin to see how the police personality is formed.

- While making an arrest for domestic violence, the wife turns on the officers and attacks them, stating that she loves her husband. The victim has been beaten so badly that one eye is swollen shut and she has broken ribs.
- A prostitute is beaten with a hanger by her pimp. The beating is so severe that she is hospitalized for weeks, yet during the interview by police, she states: "I deserved the beating; I didn't make any money." The victim refuses to press charges.
- An officer recovers a stolen moped for an elderly citizen. The next day, the same officer responds to a fatal accident where the elderly man was killed riding the moped that the officer recovered.
- An officer responds with lights and siren to a robbery and shooting. The officer enters the intersection on the way to that crime site and hits an innocent bystander's car, killing the occupants.
- Officers respond to a family's request to assist their son, who has a history of paranoid schizophrenia. After police arrive, the son experiences a psychotic episode and attacks officers so violently that they have no choice but to shoot and kill the son to stop the attack.

Calls for service such as these constantly challenge an officer's value system and moral sense of right and wrong. In every instance, officers responded to a call where the outcome was much different than the ideal of justice we envision. The reality is that officers are exposed to these calls on a routine, if not daily, basis, which forces them to become solitary or inoculate themselves by becoming impersonal as a form of psychological protection. Oftentimes, this isolation spills into their personal lives as described by Trompetter (1984), who notes that this solitary solidarity can destroy a marriage or foster alcoholism and/or poor physical health (p. 535).

Skolnick (2004) states that there are two components of the police officer's working personality: danger and authority. The element of danger relates to suspiciousness, and the element of authority is associated with enforcement of the law (p. 101). Blau (1994) argues that there are two distinct personalities when it comes to policing, which he describes as the public persona and the private persona. The public persona is one that has been defined by the media, yet the American public believes police should be perfect. The private persona is one where officers keep to themselves and let very few people in (pp. 39–40). A better explanation of Blau's description is called a biphasic personality where officers perform and act very official when at work and when alone let their hair down. The problem with letting their hair down is that it only occurs when there is no fear that they will be viewed as weak.

THE IMPACT OF GENERATIONAL DIFFERENCES

Finally, there is one piece of the police personality that is rarely discussed—generational differences in policing and their impact on the police officer's personality. Today, American policing is going through a changing of the guard. The famed police author Joseph Wambaugh described the new officers in the 1970s as *The New Centurions*. The term *new centurions* describes a changing of the guard or passing of the baton from the old to the new. This changing of the guard occurs roughly every 20 to 25 years.

The new centurions in the 1970s were known as baby boomers and are nearing retirement today. They were born between the years 1946 and 1964 (Lancaster and Stillman, 2002) and were influenced by the antiwar demonstrations of the 1960s; the proliferation of drugs; the civil rights movement; the riots of Detroit, Watts, and Newark; the assassinations of President John F. Kennedy, Dr. Martin Luther King Jr., and Senator Robert Kennedy; and the Warren Court in regard to social change and police conduct with such decisions as *Mapp v. Ohio, Miranda v. Arizona, Terry v. Ohio, Brady v. Maryland,* and *Escobedo v. Illinois* (Thomas, 2011). In essence, there was a social revolution, and the baby boomers were the change agents. Baby boomers have been described as revolutionaries, and in the 1970s, those who entered policing found an institution that was highly conservative. Oftentimes, baby boomers clashed with police on college campuses and in the marches of the 1960s. In many instances, there were clashes because of the contrasting belief systems: the tolerance and acceptance of the baby boomers versus the conservative views of the police establishment.

Today, the new centurions are from Generation X, born between 1965 and 1976, and Generation Y, born between 1977 and 1991. What is important in understanding this new generation of officers is their uniqueness. Gravett and Throckmorton (2007) describe Generation Xers as the generation with the highest number of divorced parents and dual-income families and reared as latchkey kids. As a result, they learned very early to fend for themselves and become independent. The three factors that shaped their belief system are (1) world events as seen on television, (2) peer values and views, and (3) a handful of respected coworkers (pp. 39–42). In contrast, Generation Y is 60 million strong and three times the size of Generation X. Generation Y grew up with dual-income parents, divorces, and day care. However, the parenting styles were different. Time outs became the norm, and spanking was considered child abuse. Parents protected their children from the realities of the world. Technology has had the greatest impact on this generation (pp. 44–46).

Teenage Research Unlimited notes that today more than 80 percent of teenagers have Internet access, whether at home, school, work, a friend's home, or the library. A recent study by the Fortino Group further predicts that current 10- to 17-year-olds will spend one-third of their lives (23 years) on the Internet (The Kellogg School of Management, n.d.). Why is this important in the realm of policing? Because both Generation Xers and Yers are influenced by technology; spend much of their time playing video games; text instead of talk; and have few problem-solving skills because of their parents' lack of intervention. However, policing is all about problem solving and using common sense to assist in the resolution of most problems since the majority of calls for service are not crime related.

In informal interviews conducted with officers who are baby boomers, they describe Generation Xers and Yers as not having much patience or the ability to problem solve. In fact, baby boomers describe the interpersonal skills of Generation Xers and Yers as minimal, with the end result being conflict and ultimately jail when it could have been averted. In response to the baby boomers' concern regarding problem solving, they have to be reminded that problem solving and the development of interpersonal skills is something that happens over time. When teaching in the academy, I advise police recruits of the following: "It takes about five years of ass whippings before you realize that there is another way. You want people to respect your badge and the power associated with being a police officer. However, what you learn is that you have to respect them, and the badge means nothing if there isn't a human being behind it."

Brand (1998) argues that the future of policing is dependent on those who are willing to be dedicated, professional, and upgrade their knowledge and skill levels on a continuing basis (p. 3). To this end, Brand conducted a survey of 71 Generation Xers who were criminology students attending Florida State University to assess the respondents' views in three areas: personal values, employment expectations, and job benefits. Brand concluded that Generation X has different values when it comes to off-duty lifestyle, honesty, and substance abuse and describes his findings as disturbing.

- Thirty percent of the respondents noted that their personal life should have no bearing on their professional life (p. 9). The concept of being a cop 24 hours a day does not fit with this group, which is contrary to the professional standards and ethics of policing. One would have to surmise that if an officer were arrested for drunk driving or domestic violence, it would be acceptable behavior because the violations of the law were committed while he/she was off duty.
- Twenty-eight percent of the respondents believe that someone with a felony arrest record would make a good law enforcement officer (p. 10). From what the respondents believe, a candidate's background has no bearing on their ability to do the job, let alone the agency's credibility within the community.
- Thirty-one percent of the respondents would not leave a party if marijuana were being served (p. 10). This is interesting because the off-duty officers would clearly be in violation of their oath of office and failing to enforce the law. However, this supports the belief of Generation Xers that their off-duty time is their own and that they are not beholden to the profession or their oath of office when off duty.

With that said, is there really a difference between the baby boomers and Generations X and Y? The real difference is in the norms and value systems that each group brings to the table. Police officers who are baby boomers can be closely identified with the hippie generation where the slogan was "Make love not war." The era was also associated with drugs and attempts to legalize marijuana. With this type of influence in their lives, baby boomers still choose to use alcohol over illegal substances such as marijuana. Is it possible that Brand would have received the same results if he had done this same study with 1970s criminology students?

In analyzing the generational differences, one would have to conclude that there is very little difference between the baby boomers and Generations X and Y. It is more about the new centurions transitioning to policing and developing a police personality, which has remained constant over the past 60 or 70 years. The generational differences may or may not have an impact on the profession; however, they are another piece of the police personality that must be accounted for.

CONCLUSION

The police personality does exist, but it is not innate. It is developed over time beginning with academy training; successful completion of the field-training program; constant exposure to calls for service and dealing with the public at its worst; outside stressors such as money; agency politics; family demands; peer pressure; a sense of duty to the community and fellow officers; ethical concerns and decision making; and through all of this, a need to literally cover their asses (see Diagram 2-2). Trompetter, Blau, and Skolnick describe isolation/solitary solidarity as a form of inoculation or protection of an officer's psyche. It is the impact of all of these things that creates the following personality traits: cynicism, suspiciousness, loyalty, secretiveness, prejudice, authoritarianism, dogmaticalness, efficiency, insecurity, and honorableness (Blau, 1994; Niederhoffer, 1967; Reiser, 1972; Schmalleger, 2005; Skolnick, 2004). At the beginning of this chapter, you were presented with two hypotheses, and you were asked to select the one you believed to be most accurate. The data and discussion in this chapter support hypothesis number one.

Hypothesis 1: The police personality is a myth because police officers come from many backgrounds with varying educational levels, life experiences, and

Diagram 2-2: Components That Influence the Development of the Police Personality

socioeconomic status. Yet what make the personality unique are the officers' shared experiences.

Finally, this chapter is a great stepping stone for chapters 3 and 4 in which you will have an opportunity to experience the impact that critical incidents have on every aspect of an officer's life. The one thing that will stand out is the loneliness and lack of trust that each officer has felt.

REFERENCES

Abel, R. L. (2006). *The black shields.* Bloomington, IN: AuthorHouse.

Adlam, R.C.A. (1981). The police personality. In D. W. Pope & N. L. Weiner (Eds.), *Modern policing* (pp. 152–162). London: Billing and Sons Limited.

Amnesty International. (1996). *Police brutality and excessive force in the New York City Police Department.* New York: Author.

Blau, T. H. (1994). *Psychological services for law enforcement.* New York: John Wiley & Sons.

Brand, D. (1998). *The future of law enforcement recruiting: The impact of Generation X.* Tallahassee, FL: The Florida Department of Law Enforcement.

Churchill, W., & Vander Wall, J. (2002). *The COINTELPRO papers: Documents from the FBI's secret wars against dissent in the United States.* Cambridge, MA: South End Press.

City of Los Angeles. (1991). *Independent commission on the Los Angeles Police Department.* Los Angeles: Author.

City of New York. (1994). *Commission to investigate allegations of police corruption and the anti-corruption procedures of the police department: Commission report.* New York: Author.

Dempsey, J. S., & Frost, L. S. (2010). *An introduction to policing* (5th ed.). Clifton Park, NY: Cengage Learning.

Dion, M. (1994). The multidimensionality of values conflicts in the organizational life. In S. M. Natale & B. M. Rothschild (Eds.), *Work values: Education, organization and religious concerns* (pp. 97–120). Amsterdam: Editions Rodopi, B. V.

Fritsch, J. (2000, February 26). The Diallo verdict: The overview; 4 officers in Diallo shooting are acquitted of all charges. *New York Times,* p. A1.

Gravett, L., & Throckmorton, R. (2007). *Bridging the generation gap. How to get radio babies, boomers, Gen Xers and Gen Yers to work together and achieve more.* Franklin Lakes, NJ: Career Press.

Hadden, S. E. (2001). *Slave patrols: Law and violence in Virginia and the Carolinas.* Cambridge, MA: Harvard University Press.

Herman, J. (1997). *Trauma and recovery.* New York: Basic Books.

Janis, I. L. (1972). *Victims of groupthink.* Boston, MA: Houghton Mifflin Company.

The Kellogg School of Management. (n.d.). Growing up digital: Gen Y technology usage trends. In *The risk of misreading Generation Y: The need for new marketing strategies.* Retrieved September 26, 2008, from http://www.kellogg.northwestern.edu/research/risk/geny/moreabout.htm

Kerner Commission. (1968). *Report of the national advisory commission on civil disorders: Summary of report.* Washington, DC: Author.

Knapp Commission. (1972). *The Knapp commission report on police corruption.* New York: George Braziller.

Kocieniewski, D. (1997, August 13). Injured man says Brooklyn officers tortured him in custody. *New York Times,* p. B1.

Lancaster, L. C., & Stillman, D. (2002). *When generations collide: Who they are. Why they clash. How to solve the generational puzzle at work.* New York: HarperCollins.

McFadden, R. D. (2006, November 26). Police kill man after a Queens bachelor party. *New York Times,* p. A1.

Meggitt, C. (2006). *Child development an illustrated guide* (2nd ed.). Portsmouth, NH: Heinemann Publishers.

Newman, B. M. & Newman, P. R. (2008). *Development through life: A psychosocial approach* (10th ed.). Belmont, CA: Wadsworth/Cengage Learning.

Niederhoffer, A. (1967). *Behind the shield: The police in urban society.* Garden City, NY: Anchor Books.

Rampart Independent Review Panel. (2000). *A report to the Los Angeles Board of Police Commissioners concerning the operations, policies, and procedures of the Los Angeles in the wake of the Rampart scandal: Executive summary.* Los Angeles, CA: Author.

Reiser, M. (1972). *The police department psychologist.* Springfield, IL: Charles C. Thomas Publisher.

Schmalleger, F. (2005). *Criminal justice today: An introductory text for the 21st century* (8th ed.). Upper Saddle River, NJ: Prentice Hall.

Siegel, L. J. (2010). *Introduction to criminal justice* (12 ed.) Belmont, CA: Wadsworth/Cengage Learning.

Sigelman, L., Welch, S., Bledsoe, T., & Combs, M. (1997). Police brutality and public perceptions of racial discrimination: A tale of two beatings. *Political Research Quarterly, 50*(4), 777–791.

Skolnick, J. H. (2004). A sketch of the police officer's "working personality." In B. W. Hancock & P. M. Sharp (Eds.), *Criminal justice in America* (3rd ed., pp. 100–124). Upper Saddle River, NJ: Prentice Hall.

Skolnick, J. H. (2005). Corruption and the blue code of silence. In R. Sarre, D. K. Das, & H. J. Albrecht (Eds.), *Police corruption: International perspectives* (pp. 301–316). Lanham, MD: Lexington Publishing.

Thomas, D. J. (2000). [Survey, discrimination in policing]. Unpublished survey.

Thomas, D. J. (2011). *Professionalism in policing: An introduction.* Clifton Park, NY: Delmar Cengage Learning.

Trompetter, P. S. (1984). The paradox of the squad room-solitary solidarity. In Federal Bureau of Investigation (Ed.), *National Symposium on Psychological Services for Law Enforcement* (pp. 533–535). Quantico, VA: Federal Bureau of Investigation.

U.S. Department of Justice. (2007). *Census of state and local law enforcement agencies, 2004.* Washington, DC: Bureau of Justice Statistics.

Walker, S., & Boehm, R. (1997). *Records of the Wickersham Commission on law observance and enforcement. Part 1: Records of the committee on official lawlessness.* Bethesda, MD: University Publications of America.

Wambaugh, J. (1970). *The new centurions.* New York: Dell Publishing.

Wisebud, D., Greenspan, R., Hamilton, E. E., Williams, H., & Bryant, K. A. (2000). *Police attitude toward abuse of authority: Findings from a national study.* Washington, DC: National Institute of Justice.

Police Trauma, Critical Incidents, and Stressors

INTRODUCTION

Police officers are involved in critical incidents during what would be considered a routine day. What often happens is that there are different levels of critical incidents: those that appear to be routine and those that have a profound impact on an officer's life. The routine cases would be an accident where the victims have died, a homicide, domestic violence, robbery, and/or rape. The unusual, or those that should be classified as serious, are officer-involved shootings, the loss of a fellow officer in the line of duty, the rape and murder of a child, and observing a suicide.

Regehr and Bober (2005) observe that first responders' trauma and distress are directly related to the following incidents: the death of a child, exposure to mass casualties, witnessing a violent act, being personally assaulted while on duty, life threatened while on duty, and/or the death of a coworker (p. 13). What is lost in translation is that all of these are critical incidents and in some way will have an impact on an officer's psyche because many see this type of trauma as routine.

PSYCHOLOGICAL TRAUMA AND CRITICAL INCIDENTS

In the world of policing, the most noted form of critical incident is an officer-involved shooting, but from a psychological standpoint, this may not necessarily be the case. Critical incidents are those events that overwhelm one's coping mechanisms (Everly & Mitchell, 2003). They can be classified into two categories: man-made, or as Herman (1997) notes, man's inhumanity to man, and natural disasters such as the events witnessed during Hurricane Katrina and, more recently, the earthquakes in Haiti. The underlying issue with each of these definitions is that a critical incident creates some form of stress that overwhelms an officer's sense of self-control. From a police perspective, self-control is central to the profession; without this ability, there is a perceived failure that could result in poor decision making on the job or, worse, could lead to suicide.

The question that is impossible for anyone to answer is, How much is too much? Will it be the child who is killed in an accident; a murder-suicide; an officer-involved shooting; or losing a partner in the line of duty? For some officers, it may be one of these scenarios, while for others it could be a combination of some or all of them. Take a moment and reflect on this list and attempt to determine your breaking point. During this reflection, keep in mind that there is no set standard and one's ability to cope is unique to the individual in question.

Grossman and Christensen (2008) describe the overload by using a bathtub as an analogy, noting that at some point the tub will overflow and that it is these experiences that need to be addressed (p. 274). How well an officer handles these incidents depends on a number of variables: age, years on the job, training and preparation, training to handle postincident stress, healthy coping mechanisms, support system, and the condition of the officer's personal life.

The dilemma for agency administrators is determining which incident or series of events will send an officer spiraling out of control and into crisis. It is important to note that an officer's world is not sterile or limited to the job. The officer's personal life adds to her daily stress. Some of the well-publicized personal issues that impact an officer's life are: finances, divorce, domestic violence, substance abuse/alcoholism, health concerns, depression, anxiety, and issues with anger management (White & Honig, 1995). The most difficult scenario is when an officer's professional life and personal life collide and the officer finds it impossible to reconcile either.

During such a collision, the human body may not have the ability to adapt to or turn down its response to the stress. The operational term for this inability to adapt is known as *allostasis,* or the *allostatic load,* which McEwen (1999) defines as the wear and tear of the body and brain due to chronic overactivity or inactivity of biological systems that are responsible for adaptation (p. 573). In essence, during allostasis the body is incapable of responding appropriately by turning the system on or off when needed.

The body's natural response to stress is the general adaptation syndrome (GAS), which consists of three stages: the alarm stage, which is fight or flight; the adaptation stage, in which the body adapts to a stimulus due to repeated exposure; and the exhaustion stage where the body is totally exhausted, which could lead to death, because the body is incapable of adapting to the stressor(s) (Seyle, 1984). Take a moment and think of policing and what an officer does on a daily basis. Does the job require officers to adapt, and if so how, do they adapt to the challenges? What would happen if they failed to adapt to what is viewed as routine by the profession? Some of the situations where officers must learn to adapt and control their emotions are searching buildings for a suspect(s), searching a suspect(s), handling domestic violence calls, and approaching a vehicle during a traffic stop. From the time an officer enters the academy, they are taught the inherent dangers of the aforementioned calls and, with repeated exposure, learns to adapt to the stressors.

Later in this chapter, you will have an opportunity to examine a case study of three officers, a hostage negotiator and two patrol officers, who were involved in critical incidents. The common denominator for these officers is that they agreed that their agencies prepared them to handle critical incidents. Yet with the preparation, each agency assumed that the officer understood the aftermath. The officers advised that nothing could be further from the truth. The agencies failed to understand the long-term impact these incidents had on the officers as well as their families.

The aftermath of most critical incidents is followed by some form of public inquiry. Regehr and Bober (2005) note that as a result of the public inquiry, officers and first responders are faced with a change in self-image; scrutiny by media, the public, the department, the courts, peers, and family; dealing with responses by the sources of scrutiny; and preparing to deal with the potential outcomes (p.101).

To illustrate this point, you will have the opportunity to examine three case studies. You will be provided with a detailed analysis of each incident. Before you move to the next one, take a moment and describe how one can best cope with such incidents. Examine your life and determine how you cope with stressful events. What are your coping mechanisms? Would your skill set be sufficient to overcome the psychological obstacles presented in this chapter? As you make this analysis, understand that each of us is one car accident, house fire, or violent crime away from having our lives and coping skills challenged.

Case Studies

Case Study I: Burglary of an Occupied Dwelling

Officer P is a 27-year-old white male who is engaged and living with his fiancée. He has prior military experience, having served as a military police officer in the Marine Corps for seven years with no combat experience. His only assignment at the police department before the shooting and since has been patrol. He experienced three life-threatening situations prior to this incident: one in the Marine Corps and two as a police officer. Each was resolved with verbal commands and the use of less than lethal force.

Suspect Personal Data

The suspect is an approximately 44-year-old black male who was recently released from prison after serving 15 years for Burglary of an Occupied Dwelling and Battery on a Law Enforcement Officer. The suspect spent 20 years of his adult life in prison. He had a total of 52 arrests and 15 felony convictions. It was determined in the autopsy that the suspect had been using cocaine prior to this incident. Three weeks prior to this incident, the suspect had been arrested after a violent altercation with a sergeant and officer from the same agency. After control was established, the suspect stated that the next time he encountered the police they would have to kill him. This information was never disseminated to fellow officers or placed in the police reports, nor was a safety bulletin issued for personnel.

Incident Summary: Burglary of an Occupied Residence

Officer P was working the day shift and was dispatched as a backup unit to a residential burglary in progress, involving an occupied house. The house was occupied by a female victim who was locked in her room, had called police, and remained on the line with dispatch during the entire incident. There was a second occupant who was asleep in a room on the other side of the house. The backup unit, Officer P, was first to arrive on the scene and felt that exigent circumstances existed because the residence was occupied and the status of the second occupant was unknown. He also felt it was important to enter the house to prevent potential harm to either of the occupants. Upon checking the exterior of the residence, Officer P discovered that the back door had been kicked in (Thomas, 2009, Officer P Interview).

Officer P entered the residence, and as he moved through the kitchen, he observed the suspect crouched down behind a stereo cabinet. Officer P identified himself with his gun drawn, and the suspect stood up, hoisting a bag of stolen property over his shoulder. Officer P moved to a position of contact, and at the same time, the suspect moved to close the distance between himself and Officer P. Officer P ordered the suspect to get on the floor, and the suspect stated: "I live here." Officer P attempted to use his radio to have the other units hasten their response. He was unable to call for backup but, over the open radio mike, did order the suspect to put his hands up.

At this point, the suspect closed the distance and attacked Officer P. Officer P was unable to secure his weapon, and the suspect attacked Officer P a second time. During this attack, Officer P pushed the suspect, but the suspect was braced for the officer's assault and barely moved (Thomas, 2009, Officer P Interview).

The suspect attacked Officer P a third time, pushing Officer P into the kitchen. Officer P describes this action as "two mountain goats locking horns." It was here the suspect grabbed the officer's drawn firearm. Officer P retained his firearm by snatching it from the grasp of the suspect. When Officer P snatched the weapon away from the suspect, Officer P smashed his weapon hand on the corner of the wall, which weakened his grip considerably. The suspect attacked Officer P a fourth time, again reaching for the drawn weapon. Officer P felt he could not retain the weapon if the suspect were to grab it again and made a conscious decision to shoot the suspect. Officer P fired one round, which struck the suspect center mass. The suspect fell to the floor, and Officer P secured him and called for backup and an ambulance. From the time Officer P keyed the microphone and ordered the suspect to put his hands in the air until the time Officer P came back on the radio advising shots fired, seven seconds had elapsed. The suspect died shortly after the shooting (Thomas, 2009, Officer P Interview).

Analysis of the Incident: Burglary of an Occupied Dwelling

1. Why did Officer P have his firearm drawn when he entered the building and was he justified? Officer P was entering an unknown situation. He knew the homeowner was there and possibly in danger and that the suspect was in the house as well. His firearm was drawn for protection.
2. Could Officer P shoot the suspect because he was located in the house and committing a felony? No. The mere fact that a suspect is committing a felony does not permit an officer to use deadly force. In order to discharge his firearm, Officer P or the residents of the house would have to be in danger.
3. Why didn't Officer P holster his weapon as the suspect refused to follow his verbal commands and attempt to subdue the suspect with empty hands? Even as the suspect moved closer, Officer P was not sure if the suspect was armed. Oftentimes suspects have a weapon such as a knife that is hidden and wait until they get close to draw the weapon and attack the officer.
4. Why didn't Officer P holster his weapon when the physical altercation started? At this point, it was physically impossible. In the interview, Officer P advised that he considered reholstering his weapon on several occasions but was hampered by fight or flight and an inability to perform fine motor skills. The fine motor skill in question was securing the two snaps on his holster. In addition, the entire incident only lasted seven seconds and concentration on anything other than the suspect and protecting his drawn firearm could have cost Officer P his life.
5. Was Officer P justified in using deadly force to stop the encounter? Yes. The suspect left Officer P with no choice. Officer P believed that after smashing his hand against the wall he could not defend his weapon against another attack.

Based on the suspect's level of aggression, Officer P believed that if he were to be disarmed, the suspect would shoot and kill him and possibly the residents who were in the house. Officer P shot the suspect to stop the threat and in defense of himself and the residents.

The Aftermath

Immediately after the shooting, backup arrived and the house was secured. The victim identified the suspect as the burglar. Officer P walked outside and collapsed on the fence in exhaustion. Officer P's sergeant arrived and had the officer sit in his patrol car while he directed personnel at the scene. Shortly after the officer was seated in the sergeant's patrol car, the chief of police arrived on scene with the internal affairs captain. The chief looked at Officer P and stated: "It's going to be alright. Well, I don't mean it's gonna be alright, it's not gonna be alright" and walked away. Officer P was shocked and horrified stating: "Oh fuck, as far as the press is concerned, a white police officer just shot and killed an unarmed black man, and I've got no backing from the department (Thomas, 2009, Officer P Interview)."

Stressors

Immediately after the shooting, Officer P was placed in the custody of his sergeant, and his gun belt with his firearm was taken intact as evidence. Officer P states that he was treated as a homicide suspect, not as an officer involved in a shooting while defending his life or that of another. To solidify his beliefs, the agency requested a DNA test, and when he asked why, the crime scene investigator stated: "You are a homicide susp," stopping just short of calling Officer P a suspect. Officer P states that the department added insult to injury by reading him his Miranda Rights, asked him to sign a waiver, and had a detective interview him. This all took place immediately after the shooting, without regard to his injured hand. Even more damning, he was interviewed in the same room where he had interviewed suspects for rape and murder (Thomas, 2009, Officer P Interview).

After the interview, he was sent to the hospital, and upon his return, crime scene investigators decided they needed his uniform shirt as evidence and took it. This was a mute point because the shirt had been contaminated by hospital personnel, offering no credible evidence if in fact he were a suspect in a criminal case. Finally, Officer P was placed on administrative suspension. The agency took his police credentials and advised him that he had no police authority. In addition to the suspension, they did not replace his firearm (Thomas, 2009, Officer P Interview).

Officer P's anxiety level increased tenfold based on the treatment he received by the agency immediately after the shooting. In addition to his treatment, he observed the administrators as they argued, not knowing how to proceed with the investigation. To make matters worse, Officer P left the station feeling as if he were a homicide suspect and not a police officer who had used deadly force justifiably. Based on his assessment and observations, Officer P felt the agency had discarded him pending the outcome of the investigation. In essence, they were about covering themselves, and to hell with the officer (Thomas, 2009, Officer P Interview).

Psychological Symptoms

Officer P stated that he experienced the following psychological symptoms: sleep disturbances, suicidal ideations, invasive thoughts about the shooting, distress from external cues, irritability and anger, hypervigilance, and avoiding discussion of the incident with fellow officers. In fact, every time a fellow officer attempted to congratulate Officer P or discuss the shooting, it increased his anxiety level; the intrusive thoughts began along with reliving the incident (Thomas, 2009, Officer P Interview).

These symptoms lasted approximately five months, yet he only saw the psychologist on seven occasions during the first two months after the shooting. Officer P felt after the seventh session that the department psychologist had nothing else to offer. Since Officer P's symptoms lasted longer than three months, he suffered from chronic post-traumatic stress disorder (PTSD), which went untreated for approximately three months.

Psychological Services

Officer P was referred to the department psychologist the day after the shooting. However, there was no critical incident debriefing, which would have assisted in his adjustment. Officer P had personal knowledge of the department psychologist because the psychologist was responsible for the psychological screening during Officer P's preemployment process. Officer P discovered the following as treatment began: there was no common ground between the officer and the psychologist, which meant that Officer P did not trust the department psychologist; Officer P was protective and guarded and did not disclose everything during his sessions, such as suicidal ideations, hypervigilance, high anxiety levels, and the need for antianxiety medication; Officer P felt that if he disclosed any of these issues, he would be deemed unfit for duty and never get his credentials back. Officer P never lost sight of the fact the psychologist was the department's psychologist and feared there would be no confidentiality (Thomas 2009, Officer P Interview).

Support System

At the time of this incident, Officer P was engaged and is now married. He credits his fiancée for saving his life and called her the glue that held him together. He described his psyche as a piece of clay in a hot room melting away and his fiancée as the artist who kept reattaching the pieces as they began to slide from him. When he stopped seeing the department psychologist, he looked to her for comfort and assistance and states that this incident almost destroyed their relationship noting:

1. Problems arose between Officer P and his fiancée where they both became irritable and argued frequently. This had never happened before this incident.
2. She began to fear he would be injured or killed when he returned to work, and this became a constant source of discussion in the house.
3. Because she acted as Officer P's sounding board, she began to exhibit symptoms associated with PTSD.

4. The department did not offer anything for his fiancée in the form of counseling. The department psychologist allowed them to see him as a couple, but this was futile.
5. They looked to each other to resolve the matter. (Thomas, 2009, Officer P Interview).

Reconciling the Shooting

Officer P stated that he replayed the shooting a million times in his head in an attempt to determine what he could have done differently. He finally came to the conclusion that he had no other choice. The one positive issue that came out of the therapy is that the psychologist made the following observation: "Officer P, what right do you have to allow others to die? Just think if you had not done what you did. Others would have been in danger: the two residents, your fellow officers who arrived as backup, and anyone else the suspect may have encountered. If it weren't for you, who knows what could have happened." This discussion is what allowed Officer P to begin reconciling the incident. This incident also changed Officer P; he has become much more aggressive. In fact, he states that he does not like the officer that he has become. It is because of this that he left law enforcement (Thomas, 2009, Officer P Interview).

Case Study II: Barricaded Gunman

At the time of the incident, Officer H was a 38-year-old black male, engaged and living with his fiancée and her 16-year-old son. He had 16 years of law enforcement experience, spending most of those years on the street in patrol. His prior police experience included SWAT, field-training officer, lead instructor at the academy in defensive tactics and firearms, and violent crimes detective. At the time of this incident, he was a member of the hostage negotiation team and worked the midnight shift patrol; to his credit, he had successfully negotiated with 15 suicidal individuals without injury or death. He has never been involved in a shooting and advises that he has been involved in so many critical incidents over the years that they are too numerous to count (Thomas, 2009, Officer H Interview).

Suspect Personal Data

The suspect was a 25-year-old white male with no arrest history. However, he did suffer from mental health problems and was taking Prozac to deal with depression. Two weeks prior to the incident, Officer H responded to a domestic disturbance at the suspect's residence. The neighbors called in response to an argument that the suspect and his girlfriend were having. There were no signs of violence, and no arrest was made. However, before Officer H cleared the call, the suspect stated that he would commit suicide before he would allow police to arrest him. Officer H discussed the issue further, and it was determined that the suspect did not meet the criteria to be taken into custody and evaluated (Thomas, 2009, Officer H Interview).

Incident Summary: Barricaded Gunman

Officer H was working the midnight shift and during the night in question heard a number of calls dispatched regarding a suspect who pulled a gun on his ex-girlfriend in a local bar. Later, the suspect was observed at her apartment where he fired multiple rounds through the ex-girlfriends front door and fled. Finally, his car was located at a local apartment complex, and it was unoccupied. Canine was called, and a search of the area was initiated. The canine picked up the suspect's scent, which took the units two miles from the car into a local park. Officer H was on the perimeter with a number of other units to keep the suspect from escaping or doubling back and leaving the scene in his car.

One officer was in the parking lot where the suspect exited an apartment and approached his vehicle. The officer challenged him, and the suspect turned, pointing a gun at the officer. The officer fired two rounds missing the suspect, and the perimeter units closed in on foot. The officer who challenged the suspect and fired the rounds was unable to communicate because his portable radio failed. In fact, the perimeter units had no idea the officer was there.

As Officer H approached the parking lot with a SWAT team member at his side, they observed the suspect sitting in his car with a gun. Officer H's role changed from tactical to hostage negotiation in an attempt to diffuse the situation. The negotiations began at approximately 4:00 A.M. with the suspect seated in his car with Officer H and the SWAT team member approximately 20 feet away. The suspect stated that he had nothing to live for because his girlfriend left him. The suspect wanted Officer H to have his girlfriend come to the scene, and the request was denied. Every attempt was made to get the suspect to reconcile the incident, and he refused. The negotiation process went on for three and a half hours. The suspect stated: "When the sun comes up, I am going to kill myself." He even asked Officer H if the officer thought the bullet would hurt. As the sun came up, the suspect took the gun, put it to his chest, and pulled the trigger, firing one round into his chest, which exploded his heart upon impact (Thomas, 2009, Officer H Interview).

Analysis of the Incident: Barricaded Gunman

1. Why didn't Officer H take the suspect into custody the first time they met when the suspect advised he would commit suicide before he would ever allow himself to be arrested? At the time of their first encounter, the suspect did not meet the criteria of a danger to himself or others. Without meeting one of the two criteria, he could not be mentally evaluated.
2. Did Officer H remember the suspect once he arrived on the scene and saw him in the car? No, it wasn't until after the incident and Officer H did some research that he recalled the suspect from the first incident.
3. Where were the rest of the SWAT and hostage negotiation team members? Both teams had been called out, but it takes approximately 45 minutes to get them to a scene and up and running.
4. Why were they so close to the suspect? They stumbled upon the suspect sitting in the car; it was not planned. Since the negotiation process was verbal and there were no phones or radios, they had to be relatively close to communicate.

5. Were Officer H and the SWAT team member aware of the officer who fired the two shots at the suspect? Because the officer remained hidden behind cover and his radio failed, they were not aware of his existence until after the incident. However, it was a matter of contention during the negotiation process, and the suspect feared that he would be killed if he gave up peacefully because of the shots that were fired.

6. How did Officer H know the suspect was taking Prozac? Officer H inquired about the use of drugs and/or alcohol. The suspect admitted he was taking Prozac and had been drinking that night. The autopsy confirmed the suspect had a blood alcohol level of 0.16, twice the legal limit, and there was evidence of Prozac.

7. Did Officer H attempt to stop the suspect as the sun came up? He tried everything from yelling the suspect's name to a last ditch effort to get the suspect to think of his mother. The suspect stated: "She will understand."

The Aftermath

After the shooting, Officer H and the SWAT team member approached the vehicle, secured the suspect's firearm, and called for an ambulance, which was standing by. The scene was secured by officers on the perimeter, and Officer H was complimented by his peers for a job well done. When he arrived back at his patrol unit, he collapsed from fatigue and began crying, thinking he had failed. He pulled himself together, returned to the station, and entered the suspect's weapon into evidence and completed his report of the incident (Thomas, 2009, Officer H Interview).

The psychologist was called for a debriefing but stayed 15 minutes, telling the group that he had to go to work to begin seeing his clients. Officer H stated that no one understood; even the psychologist walked out, and everyone else spent their time telling him how he should feel. Officer H experienced the following symptoms in the days to come: shortness of breath, nausea, severe cramps, sleeplessness, nightmares, and muscle spasms. This response is normal and associated with the fight-or-flight syndrome (Thomas, 2009, Officer H Interview).

Stressors

Officer H felt that no one understood him, and he felt abandoned by his fellow officers and the department because no one had ever been in this situation. Officer H found that even when those he trusted asked how he was doing, they answered for him and did not want to hear his pain and anguish. In fact, they cut him off before he could respond. His fiancée did not understand and dismissed the incident by stating: "All I care about is that you came home in one piece; to hell with the suspect." In every police shooting, an officer must see the psychologist and be cleared as fit for duty before he can return to work. However, in this case, Officer H did not have to see the psychologist and returned to work the next night (Thomas, 2009, Officer H Interview).

Although he was suffering, the problem of fit for duty was an issue for Officer H because he was well respected and feared he would be seen as weak if he went to the psychologist. He replayed the incident a thousand times in his head looking for the key or an answer that would stop the suicide; there wasn't one. Two weeks later, Officer H was called to another barricaded gunman and was pinned down behind a patrol car while the suspect fired multiple rounds striking the patrol car. After this incident, Officer H's symptoms intensified with the addition of bouts of uncontrolled anger. Even after this incident, the department did not require Officer H to see the psychologist, and he was ordered back to work the next night (Thomas, 2009, Officer H Interview).

Officer H remained on the team until he retired and continued to respond to suicides and barricaded gunmen. However, before he could respond to these incidents, he would have to throw up and then call his fiancée to get some reassurance. He retired five years after this incident, but prior to retiring, he had successfully negotiated another 15 incidents. Oddly enough, Officer H never discussed this incident with the SWAT team member, and it is unknown if the SWAT member experienced any of these stressors (Thomas, 2009, Officer H Interview).

Psychological Symptoms

Officer H stated that he experienced the following psychological symptoms: sleep disturbances, invasive thoughts about the shooting, distress from external cues, irritability and anger, hypervigilance, a sense of failure, and avoiding discussion of the incident with fellow officers. In fact, every time a fellow officer attempted to congratulate Officer H or discuss the incident, it increased his anxiety level, and the intrusive thoughts began along with reliving the incident. It may seem unusual that Officer H would be congratulated for failing to prevent the suicide. However other officers saw it as a win-win because Officer H prevented the situation from going mobile and injury or loss of life to others who were present during the incident. Officer H did consider suicide. He states: "I just wanted this to be over. I was in pain and my sense of failure was manifesting itself in every aspect of my life." Since Officer H's symptoms lasted longer than three months, he suffered from chronic PTSD, which went untreated for approximately one year (Thomas, 2009, Officer H Interview).

Psychological Services

In the case of Officer H, there were no psychological services offered. The only time he saw the agency psychologist was for a 15-minute debriefing that occurred immediately after the incident. The psychologist was there just long enough to discuss the details of the incident and declared the officers were fine. Regarding the alleged debriefing, the psychologist stated that he would be checking on the officers to see how they were doing. Officer H was disgusted by the psychologist's conduct and has no trust in him or his agency (Thomas, 2009, Officer H Interview).

Officer H was able to maintain some sense of normality because of his daily routine, which included working his shift, teaching at the local academy part time, and working out. Approximately one year later, Officer H began to unravel, fighting with his fiancée and brutally attacking a suspect in one incident, though he was cleared in the investigation. Officer H realized that something was wrong and asked his sergeant to place him on desk duty, citing fatigue and wedding plans as stressors. Officer H made an appointment to see someone other than the department psychologist who helped him reconcile the suicide and save his relationship. However, Officer H states that he was very guarded because he feared he would be labeled as unfit for duty and removed from the street. So he offered just enough, masking the symptoms and using the wedding as a ruse to gain insight into his problem. He states now that he was less than honest in his sessions, and the symptoms lasted for an additional six months (Thomas, 2009, Officer H Interview).

Support System

Officer H only had his fiancée, whom he married six months after he received treatment. Officer H never revealed his difficulty to any of his fellow officers or friends for fear they wouldn't understand and that it would hurt his image and standing in the department (Thomas, 2009, Officer H Interview).

Reconciling the Suicide

Officer H knew there was nothing he could have done and realized his actions that night probably saved his fellow officers as well as innocent civilians. However, the failure to save the suspect was disturbing because he had been successful in every other incident.

Case Study III: Domestic Violence

At the time of the incident, Officer S was a 29-year-old white male, married and living with his wife and child. He had five and a half years of law enforcement experience and had been on the SWAT Team for approximately three and a half years. Officer S credits SWAT training for saving his life. This incident is the first time Officer S used deadly force. Until this incident, he had been involved in one critical incident (Thomas, 2009, Officer S Interview).

Suspect Personal Data

The suspect is a 35-year-old black male who had 32 arrests; 19 of them were felonies, and only 3 of them were actual convictions. The suspect did not live in the apartment, but he and the victim are parents of a 13-month-old child. During this incident, the suspect was intoxicated and armed with a steak knife (Thomas, 2009, Officer S Interview).

Officer S Incident Summary

Officer S was working the midnight shift and responded to a domestic violence disturbance as a backup unit. The suspect was initially outside of the residence and then broke in. The victim retreated to the bathroom where she barricaded herself and their 13-month-old child and called police. Prior to police arriving, the suspect forced his way into the bathroom and broke the victim's cell phone. The victim fought the suspect off and was able to secure the bedroom door while the suspect attempted to force his way into the bedroom (Thomas, 2009, Officer S Interview).

As Officer S approached the house, he observed what he believed to be the suspect's arm holding a large knife butcher knife and immediately advised dispatch the suspect was armed with a knife. Officer S dropped to his knees, identified himself, and ordered the suspect to drop the knife. Once on his knees, he observed that the armed subject was the victim leaning on the bedroom door holding her child in one arm and the knife in the other hand. The suspect was on the other side of the door attempting to gain entry by hitting the door with his shoulder and knocking the victim away. Officer S described the door as opening and slamming shut with each attempt by the suspect. Officer S made the decision to enter the residence because of the suspect's acts of aggression, fearing that if the suspect gained entry into the bedroom, the victim and her child were in danger of serious injury or death (Thomas, 2009, Officer S Interview).

Once in the residence, Officer S moved through the living room, turned left, and observed the suspect at the end of the hallway still attempting to force his way into the bedroom where the victim and child were located. Officer S challenged the suspect and ordered the suspect to put his hands in the air. The suspect refused to comply and continued ramming the door with his shoulder. The suspect had his back to Officer S, and his hands were not in plain sight. Officer S made the decision to use his Taser, but the suspect turned to face Officer S with a steak knife in his hand and began moving toward Officer S. At the same time, the victim opened the bedroom door and began to exit (Thomas, 2009, Officer S Interview).

Officer S ordered the suspect to drop the knife, the suspect refused and closed to within 36–40 inches of Officer S before the officer fired two rounds striking the suspect in the upper left chest. The suspect took approximately two steps forward and collapsed on the floor. Backup arrived immediately after the shooting, and they secured the suspect. From the time that Officer S keyed his microphone and advised that the suspect was armed with a knife until the time the officer came back on the radio advising that shots were fired, 38 seconds had elapsed. The suspect survived the shooting (Thomas, 2009, Officer S Interview).

Analysis of the Incident

1. Why didn't Officer S wait for backup? Officer S feared that if he did not intervene, the suspect would break into the bedroom and harm the victim and/or the child.

2. Why didn't Officer S use his Taser rather than his firearm since the suspect was only armed with a knife? Officer S could have used his Taser, but the Taser is a nonlethal police weapon and may not have stopped the suspect who was armed with a deadly weapon. The choice to use his firearm was the correct choice. Officer S also realized that the minimum safe distance to stop a knife attack is 21 feet, and this suspect was between 30 and 40 inches away.

3. Why did Officer S shoot the suspect when the victim was behind the suspect? Officer S believed that if he did not shoot the suspect, the victim and her child could both have become hostages or the suspect could have turned and stabbed either one of them. His decision to shoot was done to stop the potential threat. Because he had SWAT team training and was an expert marksman, he had no fear that he would strike the victim or child.

Postshooting Aftermath

After the shooting, multiple backup units arrived. Officer S walked outside and sat against the wall and stated: "The whole world collapsed around me emotionally, psychologically, and physiologically." Approximately 15 minutes after the shooting, Officer S experienced the following physiological responses: severe cramping in the arms, shoulders, and back; rapid heart rate; tunnel vision; shortness of breath; sweating profusely; hot and cold flashes; and nausea. This response is normal and is associated with the fight-or-flight syndrome. Days after the shooting, Officer S experienced one week of constipation followed by two weeks of diarrhea, and he lost 12 pounds (Thomas, 2009, Officer S Interview).

Stressors

After the shooting, Officer S was approached by officers at the scene offering advice. It was at this point that Officer S took a stance that he was no longer a fellow officer and in fact believed that he had become a suspect. He described the situation as "me against the rest of the department." During the period immediately after the shooting, Officer S experienced a moral dilemma because he had just shot a man and believed that the suspect was dead at the time. He was also overcome with joy because he had survived the encounter. His emotional state vacillated between joy and the moral conflict (Thomas, 2009, Officer S Interview).

In addition to his mental state, Officer S was covered in the suspect's blood and feared that he might have been exposed to HIV/AIDS. He attempted to wash the suspect's blood off of his hands and was told not to because it could be evidence. Much like Officer P, there was no one at the scene to take care of Officer S and tend to his needs. In fact, Officer S was held at the crime scene for one and a half hours (Thomas, 2009, Officer S Interview).

While at the crime scene, the suspect's mother arrived and witnessed the crime scene investigators taking Officer S's picture and his firearm and duty belt as evidence. After he was disarmed, Officer S was placed back in the patrol car to sit and describes this as the single most humiliating event in his life: "Right then the department declared to the world I was guilty of a crime and no longer a police officer." Officer S was transported to the department, and his clothes were taken for evidence. The department also placed Officer S on administrative suspension, taking his police identification and advising him that he had no police authority. These actions heightened his anxiety and fear in regard to a lack of support and deepened his sense of isolation (Thomas, 2009, Officer S Interview).

In this incident, Officer S believed that the suspect was dead, and three hours later, he was advised that the suspect survived. Officer S advised that his whole perspective changed, realizing that the suspect had the ability to seek revenge and that Officer S would face the suspect in trial. To make matters worse, the state attorney's office had the ability to charge the suspect with a minimum of five felony charges, and they only charged the suspect with two counts of aggravated assault, one for the victim and one for Officer S (Thomas, 2009, Officer S Interview).

Finally, an ongoing stressor is that Officer S has been unable to share the incident with his wife, and it has had a negative impact on his relationship. His argument is and remains that she won't understand (Thomas, 2009, Officer S Interview).

Psychological Symptoms

Officer S stated he experienced the following psychological symptoms: sleep disturbances, invasive thoughts about the shooting, distress from external cues, irritability and anger, hypervigilance, a sense of failure, and avoiding discussion of the incident with fellow officers. In fact, every time a fellow officer attempted to congratulate Officer S or discuss the shooting, it increased his anxiety level, and the intrusive thoughts began along with reliving the incident. Officer S did not and has not considered suicide. He states that suicide is cowardly: "If I wanted to die, I would have let the suspect kill me and be done with it." Officer S still experiences symptoms to varying degrees and finds it especially difficult on the anniversary of the shooting or when responding to calls in that neighborhood. Since Officer S's symptoms lasted longer than three months, he suffered from chronic PTSD that went untreated for approximately three months (Thomas, 2009, Officer S Interview).

Psychological Services

Officer S was not debriefed and did not meet with the department psychologist until 12 days after the shooting. After the third meeting with the department psychologist, Officer S refused to meet with him anymore, stating that they had nothing in common. The department arranged for Officer S to meet with a second psychologist who is a retired law enforcement officer, but that psychologist was more concerned with his successful batterers intervention program than with assisting Officer S (Thomas, 2009, Officer S Interview).

Officer S had advised that he was unable to relate to the first two psychologists, did not trust the department based on its handling of the investigation, and believed that he no longer had value because he was involved in a shooting. During all of his sessions with the psychologists, Officer S was protective and guarded. He did not disclose everything, such as hypervigilance, high anxiety levels, severe mood swings, anger, a sense of failure, severe depression, nightmares, and stress. Officer S is seeing a third psychologist and states he will be seeing him for the rest of his life. Three years after the shooting, he still experiences bouts of depression and unprovoked crying. Officers in the department view him as weak and fear he will not be reliable in a critical incident. Finally, none of the psychologists have been able to assist him with his greatest concern, reconnecting with his wife. He states that she won't understand, but he admits that he has never attempted to discuss the shooting with her because he is afraid of what she might think of him (Thomas, 2009, Officer S Interview).

Support System

Officer S had a fairly large support system of friends, family, and SWAT team members. What is noticeable in this discussion is that Officer S has remained the most guarded with the people who are closest to him, offering that they won't understand. The most compelling statement that Officer S made regarding the incident is that the shooting "stripped me of my innocence." He offers that shooting an individual with the intent to kill reaches a level of violence that few in our society experience and challenges our morals as well as our sense of right and wrong (Thomas, 2009, Officer S Interview).

Reconciling the Shooting

Officer S understands that there is nothing he could have done differently. In addition, he is angry because he had to shoot another person. To say that he has completely reconciled the shooting and moved on is impossible, especially since he still experiences bouts of depression and unprovoked crying. Recently, this case went to trial, and Officer S cried while on the witness stand even after the suspect was sentenced to 20 years.

SENSE OF POWERLESSNESS

The ability to cope with critical incidents is based on a number of factors. First, take a moment and reflect on each incident. In the first case, the suspect was killed; in the second, the suspect killed himself; and in the third, the suspect lived. Yet all three officers experienced PTSD. Do you believe that the trauma that the hostage negotiator suffered was any different than the other two? The reality is no. However, the negotiator had an advantage over the other officers; he had more years of service, training, and exposure to numerous critical incidents. Nevertheless, the incident broke him down, why? There is one constant theme in each incident: the officers described a sense of failure in as much as they were unable to intervene or stop the incident before it escalated to the use of deadly force.

The emotions associated with each incident can best be described as being powerless (Herman, 1997). This sense of powerlessness is directly linked to the aftermath. All three officers were prepared to act; however, they lost all power due to the impending investigations, the failure of the psychologists, and the impact that the incidents had on their families. Regehr and Bober (2005) say it best: officers and first responders are faced with a change in self-image; are scrutinized by media, the public, the department, the courts, peers, and family; have to deal with responses by the sources of scrutiny; and must prepare to deal with the potential outcomes (p. 101).

CONCLUSION

There are three flawed assumptions within policing this organization: many departments believe that they have prepared their officers to handle all critical incidents, including their aftermath; the officers assume that the department is well prepared in terms of its ability to handle investigations and that it functions with the officers' best interest in mind; and the department trusts that the department psychologist provides best practices for its employees. The analysis of the data indicates that the issue is systemic and closely associated with the culture of police organizations. Kurke (1995) argues that the success or failure of an organization hinges on management and employees having their needs met or at least finding a healthy compromise (p. 395). In examining Kurke's argument, it is clear that police departments need to look beyond operations and take a vested interest in employees by defining the role of the department psychologist and becoming actively involved in the planning, training, and implementation of mental health services that meet the needs of employees.

REFERENCES

Everly, G. & Mitchell, J. (2003). *Critical incident stress management (CISM): Individual crisis intervention and peer support* (2nd ed.). Ellicott City, MD: International Critical Incident Stress Foundation.

Grossman, D., & Christensen, L. W. (2008). *On combat: The psychology and physiology of deadly conflict in was and in peace* (3rd ed.). Mascoutah, IL: Warrior Science Publications.

Herman, J. (1997). *Trauma and recovery.* New York: Basic Books.

Kurke, M. I. (1995). Organizational management of stress and human reliability. In M. I. Kurke & E. M. Scrivner (Eds.), *Police psychology into the 21st century* (pp. 391–416). Hillsdale, NJ: Lawrence Erlbaum Associates.

McEwen, B. S. (1999). Structural and functional plasticity in the hippocampal formation: stress, adaptation, and disease. In D. S. Charney & E. J. Nestler (Eds.), *Neurobiology of mental illness* (pp. 558–583). New York: Oxford University Press.

Regehr, C., & Bober, T. (2005). *In the line of fire: Trauma in the emergency services.* New York: Oxford University Press.

Seyle, H. (1984). *The stress of life* (Rev. ed.). New York: McGraw Hill Companies.

Thomas, D. J. (2009). [Barricaded gunman: Officer H interview]. Unpublished raw data.

Thomas, D. J. (2009). [Burglary of a residence: Officer P interview]. Unpublished raw data.

Thomas, D. J. (2009). [Domestic violence: Officer S. interview]. Unpublished raw data.

White, E. K. & Honig, A. L. (1995). Law enforcement families. In M. I. Kurke & E. M. Scrivner (Eds.), *Police psychology into the 21st century* (pp. 189–206). Hillsdale, NJ: Lawrence Erlbaum Associates.

Critical Incident Stress Management/Psychological Services

INTRODUCTION

In chapter 3, you had the opportunity to examine the critical incidents of three officers. The chapter closed by stating that the agencies prepared the officers to handle the incidents; however, the officers were not prepared for the aftermath. In fact, they described the aftermath as creating a sense of powerlessness. In essence, they were no longer in control of their personal or professional lives. What stood out were the issues that each officer had with the psychological services as well as the agencies' lack of sensitivity to each officer's needs. Here you will have the opportunity to examine psychotraumatology, the police personality, the inherent conflicts the officer has when receiving such services, and the best practices in psychological services for police, all of which directly reference the officers written about in chapter 3.

THE POLICE PERSONALITY

There is no police personality that is defined by the subculture (McNamara, 1999). The police personality is defined by two aspects of one's life—the first is environment, and the other is the socialization process. The socialization process is where a new officer assimilates into the police subculture. This transition challenges one's traditional belief system to establishing the aforementioned traits, which are essential in an officer's survival.

Examine the following traits and ask yourself what an officer would be like if they did not possess them: suspicious in nature, having some degree of paranoia, displaying authority when necessary, and having some degree of cynicism. All of the traits can be summed up in one word, *control,* which provides an outward persona of confidence to the public, colleagues and, in many cases, an officer's loved ones. Let's go back and examine each of the officer's comments regarding the aftermath of the respective incidents. The problem they all had was that they did not trust the agency or the psychologist because they believed that the psychologist was loyal to the agency, not the officer. The question is whether there is any truth to this belief system or whether the officers were being paranoid. Officers view the administration with some degree of skepticism and fear that the administration will not support decisions officers have made on the street. This is not without some merit because they have observed disciplinary action or a lack of backing in similar situations, which creates an us-versus-them mentality. This assertion is supported by Collins and Gibbs (2003) who note that one of the greatest sources of stress in policing can be found within the organization. What we have to understand is that regardless of the facts or past tendencies of the administration, during a crisis the officer's perception is his or her reality.

With all of the variables in place now, imagine the magnitude of each of the incidents in chapter 3 where someone's life weighed in the balance. Each officer sensed that he had failed because he was not able to prevent the incident before it resulted in the loss of life or serious injury. Couple that sense of failure with the knowledge that a psychologist has the power to declare an officer unfit for duty or have the officer reassigned to desk duty for an indefinite period of time. What will their peers think? Such actions would indicate to peers that an officer in this situation is weak mentally and cannot be trusted. Officers in the case study failed to recognize that in order to facilitate recovery, they needed to acquiesce and trust a system they had come to distrust (Greene, Heilburn, Fortune, & Nietzel, 2007; Larcombe, 2007). As the officer's worlds collide, what are the options? How does one end the pain and mental anguish?

PSYCHOTRAUMATOLOGY

Officers P, H, and S presented a number of stressors and symptoms, which were ultimately diagnosed as post-traumatic stress disorder (PTSD). From a diagnostic standpoint, PTSD is a fairly new disorder designation. However, similar symptoms can be traced back to at least the 1800s when what was then called *hysteria* was described (Goetz, Bonduelle, & Gelfand, 1995; Hergenhahn, 2008). Anderson (1999) provides a detailed history regarding the various terms associated with the cluster of symptoms we know as PTSD. Her history is exhaustive, including versions from shell shock (Word War I), battle exhaustion (World War II), stress disorder, post-sexual abuse syndrome, survivor syndrome, and battered wife syndrome to finally PTSD, first included in the American Psychiatric Association's *Diagnostic and Statistical Manual of Mental Disorders,* 3rd ed., in 1980.

Posttraumatic stress disorder is classified in the American Psychiatric Association's *Diagnostic and Statistical Manual of Mental Disorders Text Revision,* 4th ed. (*DSM–IV–TR*), as an anxiety disorder. Below is a list of abbreviated diagnostic criteria obtained from the *DSM–IV–TR*:

a. Symptoms occur as a direct result of exposure to traumatic stressors, which overwhelms one's ability to cope usually; involves direct personal exposure to actual or life-threatening events or witnessing such events, and the person's response to the events must involve intense fear, helplessness, or horror.
b. The incident is persistently reexperienced in a number of ways often described as flashbacks.
c. The individual attempts to avoid activating stimuli, which were not present prior to the incident, and experiences general numbing of one's affect.
d. Persistent symptoms of increased arousal, which were not present prior to the incident.
e. Must experience the symptoms outlined in b and c for a time period that exceeds a month.
f. The symptoms cause clinically significant distress or impairment in social, occupational, or other important areas of an individual's life.
g. PTSD is specified as acute if the symptoms last less than three months, chronic if the symptoms last three months or more, and with delayed onset if the symptoms occur at least six months after the incident (pp. 467–468).

Officers' Stressors Revisited

Officers P and S were both involved in shootings, and their experiences were almost the same, yet they worked for different agencies. Imagine being involved in a shooting and then having so little faith in your agency that you fear it will botch the investigation. In both instances, the officers were treated like they were suspects. In the case of Officer P, when the agency demanded DNA, the crime scene investigator as much as called the officer a homicide suspect. Finally, both officers were suspended along with their police power, and their firearms were taken away. Within five days they were reinstated, but the internal investigation was continuing. How long should an investigation such as this last? The reality is that it should be completed as soon as practically possible unless there are some mitigating circumstances—for example, the evidence does not support the officer's recollection of the incident. However, in each case, the internal investigations for these shootings lasted approximately six months, even though both had been cleared by a grand jury. In their interviews, both officers described a sense of helplessness and fear in regard to the internal investigation, because they could be terminated if it was determined that they violated department policy. Imagine the anguish and suspicion each officer lived with daily and the impact it had on their decision-making on the street. They feared being second-guessed at every turn and described working as a living hell until the investigation was complete.

Although both shootings were similar, Officer P and Officer S had to deal with very different outcomes. Once Officer P was cleared and his symptoms subsided, he was able to pick up the pieces and move on with his life (and in this case, he left law enforcement). In regard to Officer S, his suspect lived, which meant a trial. In preparing for trial, Officer S was required to be available for a number of depositions, meetings with prosecutors, and finally trial testimony, reliving the incident again and again. In his interview, Officer S stated: "I wish I would have killed the bastard. This would all be over. I wouldn't have to relive this incident and wouldn't have to worry if the prosecutor loses the case. You know if we lose, I could face the suspect on the street again. In fact, my greatest fear is that I will be with my son and see the suspect in a store and have to shoot him again."

Officer H's incident was different in that there was no internal investigation. In fact, the agency noted that everything was done by the book and that the negotiator did an excellent job. Officer H did not experience agency conflict or lack of moral support. His stressor was the fact that he failed and the suspect lost his life. He mentally replayed the incident repeatedly to see if he could have done or said anything differently. There was no answer. This was not a typical police incident where he could have had the ability to fight and establish control. What Officer H failed to realize in his anguish was that the suspect was in control of his own destiny, and much like suicide by cop. Suicide by cop is when a suspect is unable to commit suicide and they fabricate a critical incident, usually an armed encounter, forcing an officer to kill the suspect. During the aftermath of such incidents it is determined that the suspect's weapon was not loaded and they wanted to commit suicide. For Officer H and those officers involved in such incidents, the suspect forces the officer to participate and bear witness to horrific events.

Before Officer H could come to grips with this incident, he was asked to assist in the negotiation of another barricaded gunman two weeks later. The commander's logic was that this is still fresh in Officer H's mind and he can use his past experience to resolve this situation. Officer H and another officer were pinned down behind a patrol car as the suspect riddled the car with buckshot rounds. Although this incident ultimately ended peacefully,

Officer H began questioning his psychological well-being and his physical well-being. He stated in his interview: "For the first time in all of my years of service, I began to think about my mortality and question my profession (Thomas, 2009, Officer H Interview)."

Officers' Symptoms Revisited

Each of the officers in chapter 3 described the same symptoms, which were sleep disturbances; suicidal ideations; invasive thoughts about the shooting; distress from external cues; irritability and anger; hypervigilance; and avoiding discussion of the incident with fellow officers. Every time a fellow officer attempted to offer congratulations or discuss the incident, it increased the officer's anxiety level. Intrusive thoughts came with such triggers to relive the incident. In two of the cases, Officer P and Officer H both stated that they had considered suicide. Yet Officer P and Officer H have been able to move forward and maintain a healthy lifestyle. However, three years later, Officer S still experiences bouts of unprovoked crying, irritability, and depression; has yet to reconcile the incident with his spouse; and still sees a local psychologist, even a year after the trial's completion. Officer S stated: "I will need to see the psychologist for the rest of my life. Every time I go on a hot call, I have flashbacks, and so I need a tune up. The killer in this whole thing is I still can't talk to my wife about the incident because she won't understand." If there is no resolution to these symptoms, Officer S may well be bound for divorce, self-harm, or suicide. Take a moment to ponder: What should have been done for each of these officers?

Other Issues Associated with Police Trauma

Two other topics need to be addressed because of the very nature of policing and the closeness, or the bond, of the badge: secondary/vicarious trauma and survivor guilt.

Secondary trauma, or vicarious trauma, is something that is rarely discussed in police circles. It is assumed that only the individuals directly involved in the incident will be the ones affected. However, vicarious/secondary trauma can be experienced by anyone in a helping profession who can empathize with the event or stressors (Moulden & Firestone, 2007; Regehr & Bober, 2005). In policing, this concept can be applied to other police officers, dispatchers, and even the paramedics who respond to assist at a call.

Imagine two officers at a traffic stop during which the driver pulls a gun and shoots the contact officer. The backup officer returns fire, killing the suspect. The contact officer also dies. The series of questions or thoughts that may emerge for the officer are as follows: What did I miss? It should have been me. What could I have done differently? These questions are much like those of the officers in chapter 3. Yet they are different because the person who died was a colleague, and the officer feels solely responsible for his partner's death. If these questions linger, they are termed *survivor's guilt.* The backup officer feels guilty because he survived and the partner did not; the survivor consistently creates self-blame for failing to stop the threat, which in actuality was not something controllable.

Without healthy coping mechanisms, psychological trauma will impact an officer's personal life, possibly spurring alcoholism/substance abuse, domestic violence, divorce, and/or suicide (Clark & White, 2003; Cross & Ashley, 2004).

POLICE SUICIDE

Suicide in the ranks of policing is a dirty secret; even the word is dirty because it is viewed as a failure, a weakness, what might be called a cop out. Remember that policing is still very macho and generally considered a man's profession; real men wouldn't commit suicide, they would suck it up and move on (Clark & White, 2003). Imagine the intense pressure an officer feels during the aftermath of an incident: a sense of failure; clashing of moral values; the inability to control one's own destiny; scrutiny by the department, prosecutor, peers, media, and family; and the inability to connect with loved ones for fear that they will see him as weak. In order to stop the pain, many have chosen suicide for relief.

Police suicide is cloaked in secrecy. There is no very accurate data on the number of officers who take their lives annually. In a U.S. Department of Justice COPS newsletter, the following reasons for the inaccuracies are noted:

1. The number of suicides is relative to an agency's culture and its efforts in prevention. Compare the differences in the New York City Police Department and the Detroit Police Department:

   a. A 2002 study within the New York City Police Department for the years 1977–1996 determined that the rate of suicides in the department was less than that of the general population of New York City (Marzuk, Nock, Leon, Portera, & Tardiff, 2002).
   b. A September 2009 *Detroit News* article notes that the Detroit Police Department has the highest police suicide rate in the country, topping that of Los Angeles, Chicago, and New York (Oosting, 2009).

2. Often an agency will request that the medical examiner change the cause of death from suicide to accidental so that the officer's family can receive pension and/or insurance benefits. The death certificate might read: "accidental death while cleaning firearm."

3. Some agencies refuse to keep records of such incidents. If an agency does this, they are denying that there is a problem by ignoring the issue. In doing so, the administration has failed the officers and is turning a blind eye to a problem that could potentially become an epidemic.

The most enlightening research on police suicide is that by Aamodt and Stalnaker (2001), who completed a meta analysis of a number of studies that examined police suicide. They determined that the suicide rate in the law enforcement profession is 18.1 per 100,000, noting that this figure is 52 percent higher than the general population in the United States. However when the data for the police officers who committed suicide was adjusted to match that in the general population, the number of police who committed suicide was 26 percent less than the general population of similar demographics. They also determined that the officers most likely to commit suicide are white males, around 37 years old, with 12 years of service. Marzuk et al. (2002) support these findings in their study of the New York City Police Department and add the following to the officer profile: marital problems, alcoholism, and job suspensions (p. 2070). So how do we prevent police suicide?

CRITICAL INCIDENT STRESS MANAGEMENT

To address the immediate aftermath of traumatic events, some agencies have developed critical incident stress management teams (CISMTs). The CISMTs are composed of officers specifically trained to handle such incidents and facilitate debriefings in a group or with individuals. These officers are not psychologists but are trained to listen, be supportive, and explain the psychological and physiological responses to the event. They also have the ability to refer officers to mental health services including the department psychologist, the employee assistance program (EAP), or mental health counselor.

Critical incident stress management (CISM) is a form of crisis intervention that can best be described as psychological first aid, intended to stabilize and reduce the symptoms an officer is experiencing (Everly & Mitchell, 2003). CISM is multidimensional in that it is composed of several components with each layer designed to mitigate symptoms. CISM and critical incident stress debriefing (CISD) have been used interchangeably, but they should not be. CISD is one component of CISM, and CISD refers to small group crisis intervention composed of seven stages and performed by two CISM team members (Everly & Mitchell, 2003).

A successful debriefing provides both empathy and education. The educational process is very important because it is alerts officers to potential future bouts of anxiety and depression that they may experience and explains that those are normal and expected. It also provides the participants with information regarding additional services. The key to a debriefing may be group camaraderie, which allows each participant to understand that they are not alone. Although a debriefing is designed for a group, there are provisions for individuals such as the officers in chapter 3. Debriefing session(s) should be held as soon as practically possible (Miller, 2007; Pardy, 2005) after a critical incident. Failure to provide such services is akin to leaving an open wound untreated and allowing it to fester into a series of symptoms that could spiral into a damaging and deadly disease.

The concept of CISM is not without detractors. Boudreaux and McCabe (2000) were able to identify published studies that investigated the effectiveness of CISM and included empirical data. Their analysis found a perception that CISM was beneficial, with no data to support the outcome (p. 1096). Kaplan, Iancu, and Bodner (2001) suggest that CISM's ineffectiveness may be because it only addresses one aspect of trauma in a process negating other variables such as coping mechanisms, defensive styles, psychological history, and dissociative phenomena associated with past traumatic events (p. 826). However, an analysis of both studies shows that they address data from populations where CISM was not designed for use, including inpatient psychiatric facilities. They also failed to address the many dimensions of CISM whereby it is not a stand-alone process, but meant to be triage or short term, then providing a system of referrals.

Confidentiality and CISM

If an agency establishes a CISMT, then it must be aware of the limitations in confidentiality and the fact that sessions are not protected by state statute as are sessions with licensed mental health professionals. In addition, team members are law enforcement officers, and if the officer discloses anything criminal during a debriefing session, the CISM member is obligated to act accordingly (Angle, 2005; Archibald, 1995; Regehr & Bober, 2005). To get a better understanding of the limits of confidentiality during a CISM session, Nebraska State Statute 71–7112 (Nebraska State Legislature, 2007) states that the information obtained during such a session is not immune from discovery in a civil or criminal case just because it was obtained during a CISM session. The practice that should be adopted here is that CISM members should discuss and disclose the limits of confidentially prior to providing any services. Other than the aforementioned challenges to confidentiality, the information obtained during the interventions or debriefings is strictly confidential.

Selection of Team Members

A CISMT is not composed of mental health professionals. However, in most, if not all, cases, there will be a licensed mental health professional that has been contracted to assist in the development and training of team members. To facilitate CISM, a unique set of characteristics is required. If you think of the personality traits that most police officers have—cynicism, authoritarianism, suspiciousness, paranoia, alienation, and hostility—they are not what you would want a facilitator to display. Just think of what a session would be like if the facilitator or therapist displayed such traits. Knowing law enforcement officers as I do, they would participate in one session and the word would be out that the sessions are a waste of time and the facilitator is no good. This would be the beginning of end the program.

There are two traits that I purposefully removed from the list: loyalty and secretiveness. The Minnesota Department of Corrections (2009) outlines the following criteria for the selection of team members: two years experience in corrections, credibility with peers and management, availability for CISM responses and quarterly training sessions, strong communication skills and ability to express oneself in small and large groups, ability to be a role model for managing stress in healthy ways, and the ability to empathize with others' situations and stress reactions. If you examine the criteria, they provide for an individual who has a strong personality and a healthy lifestyle. The key to the success of such a program is the credibility of the team members.

THE ROLE OF EAPs IN POLICING

The concept of the EAP means different things to different organizations. In some cases, the model is designed to assist employees who have a drinking problem, which was the first model known as Occupational Alcoholism Programs (OAPs). The concept of an OAP is very similar to an EAP, which considers an employee valuable and almost impossible to replace when discussing years of service, knowledge, and skill set and offers that it would be cheaper to intervene rather than terminate (Rostow & Davis, 2004). From alcoholism treatment and intervention, EAP programs have grown to be defined by the FBI as post critical incident seminars that are offered immediately after a critical incident very similar to CISM (Huguley, 2000). The ultimate goals of an EAP is to assist in creating a healthy work environment through training, assessment, and referral services for employees, managers, supervisors, union stewards, and their families (Jacobson & Jones, 2010; National Business Group on Health, 2008; Roman & Blum, 1998).

Some agencies make no distinction between psychological services and EAPs and oftentimes chose one provider under the assumption that this provider will meet the needs of their employees and the organization. In essence, it is a one-stop shop, yet this one-stop shop often becomes the center of controversy because the roles of the service provider are not clearly defined. EAP was not designed as a long-term solution but was designed to provide short-term treatment or brief therapy (usually no more than six sessions), make referrals, and follow up to assess progress.

Missing in the treatment of the officers discussed in chapter 3 were two stages of psychological treatment, CISM and EAP. In all three cases, the agencies used one service provider who was responsible for everything from their preemployment evaluations to providing EAP services and fit-for-duty evaluations. In each of the aforementioned cases, there was no intervention or triage, and because of this, each of the officers suffered long-lasting psychological trauma. Just think if the supervisors had been trained to notice the signs associated with PTSD and made a referral to the EAP. What is amazing about this issue is that in each of the aforementioned case studies, fellow officers knew these officers were suffering, but no one intervened. During interviews with fellow officers and shift supervisors, they revealed that they knew the officers were suffering yet felt it was not their place to get involved and believed that it is a cross that police have to bear as part of the profession. As one supervisor stated in regard to Officer S: "He will be fine. He just needs to understand that the alternative is worse: he could be dead."

THE ROLE OF POLICE PSYCHOLOGY

Before we can begin to discuss the role of police psychology in the treatment of officers, let's revisit the discussion on the police personality. In the chapter 3 case studies, the three officers were concerned about how their peers would view them. What stands out in each case is the stigma associated with the need for mental health services. The officers feared that seeking psychological care would indicate weakness; lack of reliability in future incidents; that he/she must be suicidal; and an inherent loss of machismo, which is important in the profession. With all of the aforementioned said, you have to wonder whether there really is a police personality. The reality is that there is no such thing (Gerber, 2001).

The police personality is mythical at best and hidden behind all of the terms used to describe the police personality are fear, mistrust, and suspicion. To avoid these labels, officers hide behind the persona of the police personality in hopes that no one will notice their pain. The fear will never be displayed, and in many cases, an officer may be involved in acts of brutality.

a. As a survival mechanism within the profession to dispel rumors that he is afraid.
b. To disguise the fact that the officer is suffering from the residual effects of trauma.
c. To signal that the officer needs help when he has been too afraid to ask for help. This logic is flawed but think of it in terms of the agency having to mandate the help, which would mean the officer would not be viewed by peers as weak for seeking help on his own. In essence, this allows the troubled officer to save face.

The traits of mistrust and suspicion should be inherent in every officer. In fact, you would want an officer to have and display these personality traits because they are essential in dealing with the criminal element. These are the reasons officers stop suspects and investigate unusual activity. In addition to creating this false persona, officers have an inherent lack of trust for the administration and the use of the department psychologist. The suspicion surrounding the administration is the fear the department will use such issues as grounds for termination. The suspicion of the administration fosters an us-versus-them mentality. Organizational stress is a common theme among most officers, and in some cases, it could be described as paranoia because the officers fear that decisions made on the street will not be supported by the administration (Regehr & Bober, 2005; White & Honig, 1995). This paranoia is not without some validity; officers understand that policing is very political. In fact, it is understood that chiefs of police are only as good as their politics. So if we couple the organizational stress with a mandatory visit to the psychologist under the right set circumstances, this could easily become the great conspiracy. The department psychologist is viewed by many officers as a threat because she has the ability to end an officer's career.

Officers are aware that everything stated during sessions is confidential, yet they question if it really is. Officers also understand that confidentiality has its limits and that if it is determined that the officer is a threat, the psychologist is obligated by law to contact the administration. For all licensed mental health professionals, this is known as a *duty to warn* and is outlined in *Tarasoff v. the Regents of the University of California* (1976). The end result is that this fear interferes with successful treatment outcomes, and in many cases, an officer's symptomatology continues long after the sessions conclude (see the case studies involving Officer P and Officer H in chapter 3). In essence, because the department pays for the services, officers believe the department can dictate the outcome (Blau, 1994; Clark & White, 2003).

One major problem is that agencies fail to define the role of their mental health provider. When dealing with police, it is difficult to be a clinical evaluator, counselor/therapist, and educator without creating some conflict of interest (Archibald, 1995; Bartol & Bartol, 2008; Blau, 1994). If a psychologist wears two hats, one as evaluator and the second as therapist, then it would be impossible to determine who is the client, the agency, or the officer (Archibald, 1995). In the best of worlds, they should be separate. If an officer is to see a psychologist, then ideally it should not be the same person making the decisions regarding fitness for duty (Scrivner, 2006).

One final note regarding police psychologists. As one can surmise, police as a subculture are suspicious of anyone who is not from their circle. This concept is not limited to police officers; the same issues may arise with any group that deems itself as specialized or unique. However, each group is looking for the psychologist to share a common ground. This issue alone poses a problem for the traditional psychologist because there are few who a have a police background. It should also be noted that just because a psychologist has a police background does not mean he will be effective in treatment. This was noted in chapter 3 when Officer S was sent to a retired police officer who was a licensed mental health professional. The problem is that the therapist had become a businessperson and did not have the officer's best interest at heart.

For psychologists to be effective, they must know and understand the subculture of policing. The psychologist also needs to understand that although policing is a subculture, there are multiple subcultures within an organization and each has its own value system. They must acknowledge a client as an individual but also understand the client in the context of the group and the impact the environment has on the individual (Ivey & Brooks-Harris, 2005; Yalom & Leszcz, 2005). In therapeutic circles, there is what is known as cultural competence. If a psychologist has very little knowledge of policing, it becomes imperative they establish credibility with the officers, which can be accomplished by participating in in-service training and/or riding along with patrol. Actions such as these can address the stigma, develop trust, and establish credibility when there is little between the psychologist and the officer.

AGENCY RESPONSIBILITY

It is apparent that law enforcement agencies have a difficult time defining what is considered a crisis and when an officer should seek mental health assistance. They have one protocol that is set in stone for officer-involved shootings, yet there is very little recognition of other critical incidents. This is because, in most instances, what the general public would consider horrific, police and emergency services personnel view as routine, and therein lies the flaw in the logic. All critical incidents are just that—critical incidents—and, if nothing else, require a debriefing and possibly a referral to the department psychologist. Agency administrators should look at an officer's psyche like a cup of water; when the cup gets full, the officer has no value to the agency and is possibly a threat to herself or others.

To address these issues, agencies should develop what can best be described as a continuum of psychological care for officers who are involved in critical incidents, and the following steps should be taken:

I. After an activating event or critical incident

    a. An officer should be routed to the critical incident stress management team to educate and assess.

    b. If an individual or group, provide a debriefing; continue to assess and present options if the symptoms persist.

    c. Provide intervention services with a trained CISM intervention specialist.

    d. If a referral is needed, send the officer to an EAP for brief therapy.

    e. If need be, send the officer to the department psychologists or licensed mental health professional.

AGENCY BEST PRACTICES

In all cases, the agency needs to have two mental health providers, even if they are in the same office, with two different roles. One should be responsible for pre-employment testing, assessment, and fit-for-duty evaluations, and another should handle traditional therapy and training. This would go a long way in encouraging officers to be honest during sessions and would speed recovery. Anything short of this leaves an officer wondering who the client is, the department or the officer. In addition to establishing the guidelines, an agency should provide in-service training for its officers regarding the services and the impact of critical incidents on an officer's psyche. This should lessen the stigma associated with seeking services.

The introduction of psychological services should begin with newly hired officers. The agency should have the provider meet with new hires and their families during orientation so that family members understand the demands of the profession, the impact the profession has on families, and the changes that new officers may experience.

CONCLUSION

With all of the aforementioned services in place, very little can be accomplished if there is no system of checks and balances to recognize when an officer is in distress. Historically, first-line supervisors and command staff have not been trained regarding the best practices of leadership and supervision. The department should make every effort to train supervisors in the definition, recognition, and fulfillment of the needs of their officers during and after a critical incident. Finally, it is important for the agency to recognize that just because an officer is cleared for duty does not mean that he is ready to go back on patrol. A transition back to patrol duty may last between 24 hours and four weeks or more.

REFERENCES

Aamodt, M. G., & Stalnaker, N. A. (2001). Police officer suicide: Frequency and officer profiles. In D. C. Sheehan & J. I. Warren (Eds.), *Suicide and Law Enforcement Conference, FBI: Suicide and law enforcement* (pp. 383–398). Quantico, VA: U.S. Department of Justice.

American Psychiatric Association. (2000). *Diagnostic and statistical manual of mental disorders text revision* (4th ed.). Washington, DC: Author.

Anderson, B. (1999, March). *The psychohistory of trauma.* Paper presented at the meeting of the American Academy of Police Psychology Inc., Washington, DC.

Angle, J. S. (2005). *Occupational safety and health in emergency services* (2nd ed.). Clifton Park, NY: Thompson Delmar Learning.

Archibald, E. M. (1995). Managing professional concerns in the delivery of psychological services to the police. In M. I. Kurke & E. M. Scrivner (Eds.), *Police psychology into the 21st century* (pp. 45–54). Hillsdale, NJ: Lawrence Erlbaum Associates.

Bartol, C. R., & Bartol, A. M. (2008). *Introduction to forensic psychology: Research and application* (2nd ed.). Los Angeles, CA: Sage Publications.

Blau, T. (1994). *Psychological services for law enforcement.* New York: John Wiley & Sons.

Boudreaux, E. D., & McCabe, B. (2000). Critical incident stress management: I. Interventions and effectiveness. *Emergency Psychiatry, 51*(9), 1095–1097.

Clark, D. W., & White, E. K. (2003). Clinicians, cops, and suicide. In D. L. Hackett & J. M. Volanti (Eds.), *Police suicide: Tactics for prevention* (pp. 16–36). Springfield, IL: Charles C. Thomas Publishers.

Collins, P. A., & Gibbs, A.C.C. (2003). Stress in police officers: A study of the origins, prevalence and severity of stress-related symptoms within a county police force. *Occupational Medicine, 53,* 256–264.

Cross, C. L., & Ashley, L. (2004). Police trauma and addiction. *FBI Law Enforcement Bulletin, 73*(10), 24–32.

Everly, G. S., & Mitchell, J. T. (2003). *Critical incident stress management (CISM): Individual crisis intervention and peer support* (2nd ed.). Ellicott City, MD: International Critical Incident Stress Foundation.

Gerber, G. L. (2001). *Women and men police officers: Status, gender, and personality.* Westport, CT: Praeger Publishing.

Goetz, C. G., Bonduelle, M., & Gelfand, T. (1995). *Charcot constructing neurology.* New York: Oxford University Press.

Greene, E., Heilburn, K., Fortune, W. H., & Nietzel, M. T. (2007). *Wrightsman's psychology and the legal system.* Belmont, CA: Thomson Higher Education.

Hergenhahn, B. R. (2008). *An introduction to the history of psychology* (6th ed.). Belmont, CA: Wadsworth Cengage Learning.

Huguley, M. (2000). Joint employee assistance programs. *The FBI Law Enforcement Bulletin, 69*(11), 23–25.

Ivey, A. E., & Brooks-Harris, J. E. (2005). Integrative psychotherapy with culturally diverse clients. In J. C. Norcross & M. R. Goldfried (Eds.), *Handbook of psychotherapy integration* (2nd ed., pp. 321–342). New York: Oxford University Press.

Jacobson, J. M., & Jones, A. L. (2010). Standards for the EAP profession: Isn't it time we all start speaking the same language? *Journal of Workplace Behavioral Health, 25*(1), 1–18.

Kaplan, Z., Iancu, I., & Bodner, E. (2001). A review of psychological debriefing after extreme stress. *Psychiatric Services, 52*(6), 824–827.

Larcombe, A. (2007). Counseling isn't for the 'completely bonkers'! *Counseling at Work Journal, 55,* 16–17.

Marzuk, P. M., Nock, M. K., Leon, A. C., Portera, L., & Tardiff, K. (2002). Suicide among New York City police officers. *American Journal of Psychiatry, 159,* 2069–2071.

McNamara, R. P. (1999). The socialization of police. In D. J. Kenney & R. P. McNamara (Eds.), *Police and policing: Contemporary issues* (2nd ed.). Westport, CT: Praeger Publishing.

Miller, L. (2007). Crisis intervention strategies for treating law enforcement and mental health professionals. In F. M. Dattilio & A. Freeman (Eds.), *Cognitive-behavioral strategies in crisis intervention* (3rd ed., pp. 93–121). New York: Guilford Press.

Minnesota Department of Corrections. (2009). *Critical incident stress management: Policy number 103.090.* Saint Paul, MN: Author.

Moulden, H. M., & Firestone, P. (2007). Vicarious traumatization: The impact on therapists who work with sexual offenders. *Trauma, Violence, & Abuse, 8*(1), 67–83.

National Business Group on Health. (2008). *An employer's guide to employee assistance programs: Recommendations for strategically defining, integrating, and measuring employee assistance programs.* Washington, DC: Author.

Nebraska State Legislature. (2007). *Critical incident stress management act: 71–7112 Confidentiality of information.* Lincoln, NE: Author.

Oosting, J. (2009, September 23). Suicide rate amongst Detroit cops highest in the nation. *The Detroit News Archives,* p. 8.

Pardy, J. (2005). *Conflict management in law enforcement.* Toronto, ON: Emond Montgomery Publishing.

Regehr, C., & Bober, T. (2005). *In the line of fire: Trauma in the emergency services.* New York: Oxford University Press.

Roman, P. M. and Blum, T. C. (1988). The core technology of Employee Assistance Programs: A reaffirmation. *The ALMACAN*, 18:17–22.

Rostow, C. D., & Davis, R. D. (2004). *A handbook for psychological fitness-for-duty evaluations in law enforcement.* Binghamton, NY: The Haworth Press.

Scrivner, E. (2006). Psychology and law enforcement. In I. B. Weiner & A. K. Hess (Eds.), *The handbook of forensic psychology* (pp. 534–551). Hoboken, NJ: John Wiley & Sons.

Tarasoff v. the Regents of the University of California. 1976. 17 Cal. 3d 425, 551 P.2d 334, 131 Cal. Rptr. 14 (Cal. 1976).

U.S. Department of Justice. (2009). *By their own hand: Suicide among law enforcement personnel.* Retrieved February 3, 2010, from http://www.cops.usdoj.gov/html/dispatch/April_2009/suicide.htm

White, E. K., & Honig, A. L. (1995). Law enforcement families. In M. I. Kurke & E. M. Scrivner (Eds.), *Police psychology into the 21st century* (pp. 189–206). Hillsdale, NJ: Lawrence Erlbaum Associates.

Yalom, I., & Leszcz, M. (2005). *The theory and practice of group psychotherapy.* Cambridge, MA: Basic Books.

Hostage Negotiation

INTRODUCTION

Hostage negotiators are skilled in the art of defusing a crisis situation. But when the negotiator enters the arena, they have very little to say about the hand that an offender has dealt. The negotiator must adjust to the needs of an offender using these skills: active listening, empathy, paraphrasing, and knowledge. These skills provide a framework of understanding, which allows the negotiator to connect with an offender when they may be at the lowest point in their lives.

Influencing the negotiation process are officer and offender culture, mental status, willingness to resolve the situation, motivation, desired outcome, understanding of the law, and substance use or abuse—issues that make the negotiation process dynamic and ever-changing. Now explore the processes associated with hostage negotiation, including history, negotiator selection process, training, skill sets, intervention strategies, and the psychology of the hostage taker.

A BRIEF HISTORY OF HOSTAGE NEGOTIATIONS

Hostage negotiation is fairly new as a police specialty, and it was triggered by incidents in the 1970s. The 1960s and 1970s were violent times in the United States. There were a number of airplane hijackings, which fall into one of two categories: extortion or politically motivated. Law enforcement officials internationally had to negotiate with terrorists to prevent destruction of aircraft or loss of life. There were two particular incidents that set the stage for what we now know as hostage negotiation. The first was the siege and massacre of the Jewish Olympians in the 1972 Summer Olympic Games. The second incident occurred in 1973, shortly after the New York City Police Department had developed the first hostage negotiation team in the United States (Kitaeff, 2011; Louden, 2007; Strentz, 2006).

- In 1972 the Summer Olympics were held in Munich, Germany. On September 5, 1972, eight Palestinian members of the Black September terrorist organization entered the Munich Olympic Village dressed in track suits and armed with grenades and machine guns, their target the Israeli delegation. Eleven Israeli athletes were taken hostage; 2 were killed in the Olympic Village. The standoff lasted 20 hours, and the hostage takers were allowed to leave the Olympic Village with the hostages in an effort to escape by aircraft. The hostage takers were met by German police and military at the airport where a gun battle ensued, and the remaining 9 hostages were killed as well as five of the hostage takers and one police officer (Farrell, 2010; Sonneborn, 2003).
- Three of the members of Black September were captured and expected to stand trial. However, in October 1972, they were released when two Palestinian terrorists seized a German airline and threatened to blow up the plane and the 11 hostages they had taken. The German chancellor released the Munich terrorists to avoid further bloodshed (Ensalaco, 2008; Sonneborn, 2003).
- The second incident occurred in January 1973 after the New York City Police Department developed the first hostage negotiation team in the United States (Kitaeff, 2011; Louden, 2007; Strentz, 2006). This incident lasted two days and took place at John and Al's Sporting Goods after a botched robbery and the murder of a New York City police officer. This incident was immortalized in the fictional movie *Dog Day Afternoon*. The robbery at John and Al's revealed the value of the hostage negotiation process and solidified its role in American policing. Four black male suspects held 11 hostages. When police responded, they were met with a hail of gunfire where one officer was killed, two officers were wounded, and one hostage taker was wounded. The *New York Times* describes the beginning of the siege as a battleground with hundreds of rounds exchanged between the suspects and the officers. Since it was the first incident, the police commissioner described his feelings of frustration because he knew so little about the suspects and feared that as they sat waiting for a peaceful solution, the suspects could kill the hostages without interruption (Carmody, 1973). To assess their efforts at the scene, the commissioner established what he described as a think tank that consistently reevaluated the situation to assess the viability of the negotiation process. The suspects were militant Muslims and vowed to die for "victory and paradise" (McFadden, 1973). The commissioner's decision not to storm the building won out; the hostages were freed, and the suspects surrendered. This revealed the value of the hostage negotiation process and solidified its role in American policing.

During the siege, the New York City Police Department used a number of resources to assist in resolving the incident. It allowed the suspect's family members to meet with the suspects, local Baptist ministers spoke to the suspects from the armored personnel vehicle, a Muslim minister entered the building and spoke with the suspects, and the negotiators allowed a medical doctor to enter and treat one of the suspects who was seriously wounded (McFadden, 1973). That created trust and assured the suspects that they would not be killed or beaten if there was a surrender. The establishment of this trust was especially important as police had no prior credibility in that neighborhood in that era. That lack of credibility in the black community was a direct result of acts of brutality perpetrated earlier by police in the community on suspects who were guilty of crimes far less harmful. The success of this incident's handling set the stage for what we now know as hostage negotiation.

TEAM MEMBER SELECTION AND STRUCTURE

If you were in charge of creating a hostage negotiation team for a police agency, what criteria would you establish for the selection of team members? How would your team look? Is diversity of the team important; do you need members of different age groups, ethnicity, religions, and specialties? Or is the most qualified applicant the best for the team, and do you expect to teach them everything they need to know about diversity? Would you want someone who is an experienced SWAT team member, so that she understands the tactical aspect of hostage situations? Or would the best team member be someone who has a background in psychology or mental health?

The personality traits of a good negotiator include excellent communication skills, the ability to adapt to changing dynamics, capacity for sympathy, self-confidence, emotional stability, extroversion, and a liberal orientation (Gettys and Elam, 1988; Strentz, 2006). These traits exemplify the ideal candidate, but an analysis of research by Louden (2004) leaves questions as to the selection and training of negotiators. Louden (2004) completed an analysis of data from 276 state and local law enforcement agencies that responded to the *Law Enforcement Management and Administrative Statistics 1993* (1995); each of these agencies employed 100 or more personnel and detailed the following regarding hostage negotiation and team member selection. Fifty-six percent of the agencies did not have a policy regarding the selection of team members, and the process for becoming a team member occurred in one of three ways: 32 percent filled the position through an agency posting, 30 percent were encouraged to apply by someone in the agency, and 32 percent presented themselves as volunteers without being prompted (p. 51).

Louden's findings suggest that the selection process in most cases is far from formal and as a result may not be enlisting people who are ideal for the agency or the community. Some agencies provided as little as 4 hours, and others as many as 250 hours of training for negotiators; the average number of training hours was 47 hours (Hammer, Van Zandt, & Rogan, 1994; Louden, 2004). Before we move on, take a moment to reflect on the selection and training of the negotiator in relation to the demands of a crisis. What happens if the negotiator suffers from a psychological disorder or is not suited for negotiations? The most successful negotiators are those who can think critically and establish a rapport with the hostage taker, and anything short of that will probably result in the loss of life. In chapters 3 and 4, there is a detailed account of a negotiator and the aftermath—even after all of his training and years of service, he was traumatized for years. Imagine what his life would have been like if there was little to no preparation.

TEAM DIVERSITY

A term which has been received negatively in policing is *hiring diversity*. It has been associated with affirmative action, promoting because of race or gender as opposed to those who are most qualified, hiring unqualified candidates, and promoting the needs of the community over those of the officers and the agency. But when it comes to hostage negotiation, diversity is necessary for the team's success. This is one area that cannot be ignored, because it is impossible for a team that is composed of one race or gender to meet the needs of all they serve. Team members and leaders need to recognize that the there are many subcultures in our country and that it is to these subcultures that we retreat during times of crises. Consider these personalities and identify what you might have in common with them: a Haitian immigrant who believes he has lost his daughter to American values, a biracial father of five who is addicted to crack cocaine, a black Muslim who murdered two police officers in self-defense, a Latino Gulf War veteran, a student who is a stalker, and a suicidal high school student who is holding classmates hostage. You will have an opportunity to visit each of these personalities later in this chapter and review the results of an experiment where negotiators, police recruits, graduate students, and high school students attempted to interact and resolve each of these scenarios.

To further stress the need for diversity, Hammer, Van Zandt, and Rogan did the first study profiling hostage negotiation teams and published the data in a 1994 article entitled "Crisis/Hostage Negotiation Team Profile." One hundred team leaders participated in the survey, and the following was a snapshot of negotiation teams: the data revealed that most of the teams were dominated by white males, with very few women or minorities; few teams had written policies regarding the selection of team members; and the training of new members lasted 10 days (pp. 8–9).

Diversity from a practical standpoint is not always ideal or possible; the hostage taker will not get to select the negotiator, nor will it always be best to assign someone as the lead negotiator who has a similar background. Thomas (2008) argues that police look at the world through a different set of glasses that are unique to the profession, and often police decision making is cut and dry based on the fact that the "law is the law," and there is only one value system from which our legal system sees proper action (p. 173). Yet the process of hostage/crisis negotiation is far from cut and dry. It is a process wrought with raw human emotion. What diversity offers are different views and understanding, where there may otherwise be none.

The demographics of the United States are changing, and to address the overall needs of the community that an agency serves, there is a clearly a need to diversify the teams. Passel and Cohn (2008) state that the U.S. population will soar to 438 million by 2050. Nearly one in five Americans then will have been born outside the United States, versus one in eight in 2005. Sometime between 2020 and 2025, the percentage of foreign-born citizens here will surpass the historic peak reached a century ago during the last big immigration wave. Finally, white Americans will no longer be the majority population in the United States as their share will drop to 47 percent.

It will be, and already is, difficult to impossible to know every characteristic of the many cultures an officer may face and have to work, or negotiate, through. So there are two things to consider when evaluating a team's needs: (1) the demographics of an agency's jurisdiction and (2) team composition, or how to best prepare for, and hire for, the cultures most likely to demand understanding from an officer or negotiator. Personally, I do not advocate selecting a member based fully on race or gender; each member must meet the standards and pass the team's selection process. But jurisdictional demographics are constantly changing, and an agency's training must reflect those changes.

NEGOTIATOR SKILL SETS

The skill sets required in the negotiation process are active listening, the use of empathy statements, the ability to paraphrase, and knowledge. To be successful, a negotiator must be adept at these skills, with the understanding that a crisis does not happen in a vacuum but is associated with one event or a series of events that create a dynamic. As important as the skill sets are, success is also dependent on the negotiator's knowledge of life's successes and failures. The good negotiators are those who have life experience as well as police experience and have the ability to apply that knowledge to the situation (Herndon, 2009; Poolos, 2007; Volpe, Cambria, McGowan, & Honeyman, 2006).

Active Listening

Active listening is defined as one's willingness and ability to hear and understand, which involves six skills for police negotiators: attentiveness to detail and the stated problem(s) of the hostage taker; remaining unbiased and nonjudgmental of the message and the hostage taker's cause, so reflecting on the information as it is presented; asking questions to clarify information, intentions, needs, and/or motives; summarizing the information by paraphrasing to confirm that the negotiator has been listening and understand the demands of the hostage taker to create rapport with someone in crisis; and sharing findings with superiors actively involved in the decision-making process. (Hoppe, 2006; Ivey, Ivey, and Zalaquett, 2010; Stamatis, 2002). Each skill set is very important. If, for example, a negotiator fails to listen to what the hostage taker/person in crisis is saying, then there is no way to move forward.

Envision a hostage taker pouring his heart out to the negotiator, with little or no feedback. What will the emotional response be? I've seen in training and in actual negotiations that the emotions are intensified: anxiety, frustration, and anger grow, often paralyzing the communications process. Such an inability to move forward is known as *circling*. Circling refers to when information the hostage taker has presented during dialogue it is not acknowledged or dealt with in an effective way by the negotiator, so that even after a change of subject, the hostage taker returns to that information, seeking recognition of it and resolution (Knudson, 1999). If the negotiator continually fails to acknowledge the problem, the communication process is destroyed; an unintentional message is that there is little concern for the hostages or a peaceful resolution.

Empathy Statements

The use of empathy statements is very important in crisis situations because it allows the negotiator to view the crisis from suspect's point of view. It has been my experience that when people are in crisis they often initially view those who are there to help as unable to understand. Some of the comments that I have heard during these encounters include the following:

- "You are a police officer; you have the perfect life; you know nothing about divorce and child support."
- "You have never been in money trouble, so how could you possibly understand?"

- "You've never thought of suicide; you can't understand my situation."
- "You have never lost your job and your family, so what would you know about this?"
- "You've never been betrayed by someone close to you."
- "I am an addict! There ain't no way in hell that you understand that because drugs are illegal, and if you'd been a junkie, you would not be a cop."
- "This bastard raped and murdered my child! What would you know about that? So I am going to get revenge, by killing him; that way, the world will be free of him. Then I am going to commit suicide, because I can't go on living. You never felt these emotions, so how could you possibly understand?"
- "The Lord God Almighty told me to come here, take these sinners hostage, and make them repent. If they fail to repent, then I have been instructed to kill them."

Rogers (1961) defines empathy as "an accurate empathetic understanding of the client's world as seen from the inside. To sense the client's private world as if it were your own, but without losing the 'as if' quality—this is empathy" (p. 284). Mead (1993) defines empathy as "the capacity to take the role of the other and to adopt an alternate perspective" (p. 27). Hogan (1969) defines it as "the ability to take the intellectual or imaginative apprehension of another's condition or state of mind" (p. 308). But a negotiator may have to de-escalate the situation first before utilizing this tactic.

Greenstone (2007) notes that there are 25 errors in the negotiation or crisis process, with the most notable specific to a lack of empathy from the negotiator. The errors include not understanding the mind-set of the other party; failure to understand the interests of the other side; not appreciating the validity of an argument; and utilizing ineffective communication skills (pp. 108–109). Greenstone's analysis shows that empathy is about meeting the suspect one-on-one, so that the negotiator and suspect have the same level of understanding. It has been described as getting into "the well" with the person. The process becomes no longer us versus them; instead, a bond is established. The offender is willing to comply with the negotiator's requests, and the negotiator responds favorably to the offender's request. Who is in control is no longer so important because they are operating in an atmosphere of cooperation and apparent mutual respect (Jones, 2000; Knudson, 1999).

Kulis (1991) identifies three categories of empathy statements—high, medium, and low—and asserts that empathy statements can be useful or harmful in any negotiation. The key is timing. Empathy statements can only be used when the stage has been set for meaningful dialogue.

High empathy statements capture the surface information and feelings, in addition to meanings and feelings below the surface. This level of empathy should be used sparingly to move stalled negotiations. This type of statement may require the negotiator to enter and share his personal life. It is important to understand, as discussed earlier, that the offender must be willing to receive this information and process it accordingly. If not, the negotiator may be seen as weak and ineffective. Here the negotiator is truly in "the well" with the offender; however, the cost to the negotiator may be personal. Example:

Offender: You have no idea what it's like. I fought for this country during the Gulf War, and it has abandoned me since I returned home.

Negotiator: I understand. I served two tours in Iraq. I lost friends and feared that I would not make it home myself. I've been home two years and still relive the acts of horror that I saw. But do you believe that killing your hostages is worth it? What about your family? They still need you. They can help; that's who helped me?

Medium empathy statements capture surface information and feelings, yet avoid in-depth probes. They go no deeper than the offender has gone and can be used repetitively without harm. Negotiations at this level are free flowing and aimed to be productive. This is where most negotiations should take place because the negotiator does not have to go deep into "the well." Example:

Offender: You have no idea what it's like. I fought for this country during the Gulf War, but it has abandoned me since I got home.

Negotiator: I couldn't possibly understand what you feel after serving in Iraq, so I am not going to pretend that I do. But I do understand that you are angry and feel betrayed and that the only way to get even is to make those who have abandoned you suffer, and you feel that revenge is your only recourse. But realize that killing the hostages will only create another set of problems for you and your family. What about your children?

Low empathy statements eliminate the offender's frame of reference from the dialogue. Low empathy statements are detrimental because the offender's point of view is completely missed. This can be damaging because, in most cases, the offender has the expectation that the negotiator can and should attempt to understand. Example:

Offender: You have no idea what it's like. I fought for this country during the Gulf War, and it has abandoned me since I returned home.

Negotiator: I understand that you fought in the war, but we need to end this. We need to get these people back to work.

Paraphrasing

Paraphrasing is rephrasing the content points of the offender's statement, not the emotion, which allows the negotiator to test her understanding of that communication (Kanel, 2002; Slatkin, 2010). In order to better understand paraphrasing, let's expand on the dialogue with the Gulf War veteran.

Offender: You have no idea what it's like. I fought for this country during the Gulf War, and it has abandoned me since I returned home. I have been denied psychological services, the war cost me my house, and I have no choice but to kill the hostages I have here at the VA.

Negotiator: I want to make sure that I understand you. It sounds like you are angry, depressed, and feel betrayed because of the losses you have suffered. You lost your home and you are in need of services but the Veterans Administration has denied your claim. If I understand you correctly, you have every right to feel as you do.

Offender: You are goddamn right, and these bastards have to die.

Negotiator: You are telling me that you are going to kill them because they are responsible and have failed you miserably and their actions destroyed your quality of life.

Offender: Man you are smart; you understand, but these bastards don't, and that is why they have to pay.

Negotiator: I understand your feelings, but before you hurt anyone, let's work through your feelings and why all of this happened.

The negotiator poses questions while paraphrasing, which gives the offender an opportunity to clarify the meaning of his statements. The skill sets are not individual components; they are intertwined because the negotiation process is dynamic and fluid. So far, we have discussed the negotiation process as one-on-one, yet if done properly, it is a team approach with several members assisting the lead negotiator. This is important because they assist in capturing critical information that may be missed by the lead negotiator. If it is a team process, there is a primary negotiator; a secondary negotiator to assist in analyzing the communication; a scribe to record contact, who initiated the contact, and the content of the conversation; and an intelligence coordinator (Regini, 2002; Terestre, 2005).

THE IMPORTANCE OF TRAINING

The necessity of training and skill development cannot be stressed enough. In their survey, Hammer et al. (1994) noted that 61 percent of the teams trained on average between one and five days a year (p. 8). I (Thomas, 2008) conducted a study with graduate students who were in the Forensic Behavioral Analysis Program at Florida Gulf Coast University. In this experiment, I wanted to determine if education alone would allow a negotiator to be successful in a crisis situation. I believed that because the students had completed a number of psychology courses, coupled with the fact that many worked in the field of criminal justice or psychology, at least 50 percent of the students would resolve their crisis peacefully. In fact, the outcome was much different. There was only a 10 percent success rate (p. 181). The students were asked, What was the most difficult thing about the exercise? Their responses were as follows: not being able to connect with the suspect because of his race/ethnicity, no control of the situation, fear of saying the wrong thing and getting the hostages killed, a lack of preparation, and feeling useless and hopeless (p. 180).

To further test the hypothesis concerning skill development and training, Thomas (2009) conducted an unpublished study with a graduating class of Florida police recruits. Unlike the earlier graduate students, this group's educational background ranged from a high school diploma to one person who had a master's degree. The most common levels of education were a four-year degree and some college but less than an associate's degree, which totaled 57 percent of the recruits. For those who attended college, most had taken at least one course in psychology, but in the academy, all had received training in human interaction, interpersonal communications, crisis intervention, and suicide (Florida Department of Law Enforcement, 2008). In addition to their classroom training, the recruits participated in several scenarios to reinforce what they learned in the classroom. Yet the results were exactly the same as the graduate students, a 10 percent success rate. The police recruits were asked, What was the most difficult thing about the exercise? Their responses were the following: no control of the situation, did not understand and could not communicate, we were stuck and could not move forward, trying to establish trust, and not knowing what to say.

The Scenarios

The police recruits and the students had been given a fact sheet detailing the information about their particular scenario. The police recruits were placed in groups of two and received the information as if they were being dispatched to a call for service. The graduate students were paired into groups of two and had an advantage because they were given their scenario a week in advance so that they could research to prepare. The scenarios were assigned at random, and to ensure uniformity, the hostage taker was the same in each scenario. As you review the scenarios, assume the role of negotiator and determine how you would resolve each of these without the use of deadly force or tactical team entry.

- **Haitian Immigrant**
  This suspect is a Haitian immigrant by the name of Richard who has lived in this country for five years. He is married and has a daughter, 15, and a son, 10. His daughter rejects everything Haitian, adopting the Anglo-American lifestyle. She practices premarital sex and is pregnant by a white male. The practicing religion of the family is voodoo, and he has taken the family hostage.

- **Biracial Father**
  This suspect is a biracial (African American and Caucasian) father of five; each child has a different mother. His name is Tom, and he is a crack addict. Tonight he has spent all of his welfare check on crack cocaine and is holding his children hostage.

- **Police Officer**
  The suspect in this case is a fellow police officer. He is a white male, and his wife is a black female; they have one child together. His name is Paul. Paul has been having problems in his personal life. His wife has tried to pinpoint the cause of the problems, but Paul refuses to discuss the matter. In fact, she describes him as obsessing over the issue for the last month. His behavior has changed in that he began drinking heavily and showing signs of paranoia. He has barricaded the doors with furniture and refuses to let his wife and child leave the house. In fact, he has locked them in a bedroom. There is no more communication with the suspect or his wife and child because he will not answer the phone.

- **Black Muslim**
  The suspect in this case is a black male who is a devoted Muslim. His name is Hayward X. He was stopped for speeding by two white police officers. Witnesses state that they saw the officers pull Hayward from the car and beat and kick him. During the assault, Hayward took one of the officer's firearms and shot and killed them both. He fled the scene and has been located on the campus of the local university, barricaded inside a classroom with 25 students. He has not responded to repeated attempts of communication by the university police department.

- **Angry Veteran**
  The suspect in this case is a Latino male by the name of Michael Hernandez. Mike is a Gulf War veteran and just returned from a second tour in Iraq. We received a call that the neighbors could hear yelling coming from the residence. Mrs. Hernandez also called the police when Mike left the house, threatening to burn the house down. Police attempted to stop him. He fled, making it back to the residence with a 10-gallon can of gas. His wife said that she and the kids were in the house, then ran in and hung up. Mike is not responding to the officers on the scene.

- **Student Stalker**

  The suspect in this case is a white male named Thomas. He is a student at the local university and is in love with another student; he has been stalking her. On this day, Thomas approached her, and they exchanged words. Witnesses state the victim called Thomas "a pig." Thomas has taken the victim hostage and locked himself in the dean's office. Upon contact by the university police department, Thomas threatened to kill the victim and then commit suicide, but stated that the victim "will suffer before she dies."

The two studies in which these situations were posed did not use actual police officers or hostage negotiators, and the findings indicated that specialized training and repetitive skill development are essential in a negotiator's success. Training should emphasize skill development that meets the needs of the community, no matter how difficult.

THE PSYCHOLOGY OF HOSTAGE NEGOTIATION

Imagine shopping at your local supermarket and having two armed suspects come into the store to rob it. During the robbery, the police arrive and the suspects are trapped in the store. The suspects have determined that the only way out is to take everyone in the store hostage. You did not know initially that the robbery was taking place, because the gunmen entered the store without announcing their intentions. However, the manager observed one suspect with a firearm and activated the silent alarm. Before the suspects could leave the store, two police officers arrived on scene, creating the hostage crisis that you are in now. As a hostage, or hostage taker, can you imagine the anxiety, fear, and anger that all are experiencing the very moment the crisis begins? In this incident, the hostage takers have one thing on their minds—escaping. Before they can do anything, they must establish control, proving to the police and hostages that they are serious and will do anything to escape (Hunsicker, 2006).

Stages of a Critical Incident

Every critical incident traverses several phases/stages before it is brought to some form of resolution. A hostage situation begins with the first officers on the scene, who may well be responsible for establishing contact and stabilizing the situation until SWAT and the negotiators arrive. It is important to note that the stages of a critical incident are not etched in stone or concrete, because negotiators are dealing with the behavior of two different groups— the hostage takers and the hostages themselves. The dynamic between these two groups is independent of the negotiation process, especially if the hostages are combative or suffer from any medical/mental health condition that may exacerbate the situation. The stages of a hostage/critical incident generally are the following:

- **Stage I/Panic:** It is the beginning of the incident and the most critical time because this is where the hostage taker is looking to control the hostages and the hostages are looking for a way out. The hostages will be in panic mode once they have been informed that they have been taken hostage. During this phase, the hostages will assess, analyze, and determine the best course of action. They will also experience fear, anxiety, anger, and a loss of control. However, for the hostage takers, it is their motive that will determine if they are actually panicking. If the hostage takers are criminals and the criminal act is interrupted, the goal is to escape. In this case, the hostage takers will exhibit heightened levels of anxiety, anger, and fear similar to the emotions of the hostages. Through this collage of emotions, they are attempting to develop a plan of action and establish control. In contrast, if the hostage takers are terrorists, the incident has been well planned, and the only behavior they can't account for is that of the hostages. It is also important to note that hostage takers may wound or kill a hostage to establish control.
- **Stage II/Uneasy Calm:** Here the battle lines have been drawn. The police have established a perimeter, and they have attempted to establish contact with the hostage takers. On the other hand, the hostage takers have secured the hostages and are in the process of developing a plan of action as well as drafting a list of demands. In the beginning, this process is very fragile, with the hostage takers wanting the negotiator to understand who is in control. The role of the negotiator here is to determine if there are injuries or if medical assistance is needed and to address other needs that the hostages/hostage takers may have. The goal is to stabilize the situation and lower the stress and anxiety levels of the hostage takers. This is where active listening begins and the negotiators establish a rapport and some degree of trust.
- **Stage III/Negotiation Phase:** Huber (2006) describes the negotiation process as give-and-take between individuals who are looking to resolve a conflict, and an essential element in the negotiation process is bargaining, which is the exchange of favors to assist in successfully resolving the negotiation process (p. 409). Bargaining is important because it provides the platform where negotiators can get a hostage released for food or medical attention. In policing, there are a number of boundaries in the negotiation process, and the first is the law. For the negotiator, it is important to know what crimes have been violated so they can respond accordingly to the hostage taker's inquiries. The variables that influence the negotiations from a law enforcement perspective are department policy, crimes committed at the scene, motivation of the hostage taker, injuries or death of hostages, willingness to negotiate/bargain, and the mental health status of the hostage taker. If this phase has been successful, then there is the potential to move to a peaceful resolution; if not, then it may require a tactical solution.

- **Stage IV/Resolution:** Peaceful resolution without the loss of life and injury is the ultimate goal of any hostage incident. If it is peacefully resolved, the hostage takers and the negotiator have found a common ground that has allowed them to move forward in the process. If the resolution is peaceful, then the hostages will be released first, followed by hostage takers' surrender. However, if the crisis cannot be resolved peacefully, then the solution becomes tactical, a last resort. A tactical solution can best be described as turning the incident over to SWAT. If the negotiations have been extensive, then SWAT will have devised an entry plan and will enter the building with two goals: safe recovery of the hostages and establishing control of the hostage takers. Control of the hostage takers can occur either by the hostage takers surrendering or by officers using deadly force in defense of themselves or the hostages. A tactical solution can occur because it is sensed the hostage takers have decided that there is no way out except murder-suicide; the hostage takers continually change demands, and those demands are impossible to meet; the stability and mental state of the hostage takers becomes more bizarre and unpredictable; the negotiations are at an impasse and the hostage takers' dialogue is repetitive, refusing to acknowledge the negotiators; or it is determined that the hostages are in immediate danger.

THE PSYCHOLOGY OF HOSTAGE TAKERS

Researchers have developed numerous categories for hostage takers. In 1976, Hacker categorized them as the crusader, the criminal, and the crazies (p. 8). Since Hacker presented his categories, the numbers and classifications have changed over the years depending on the researcher and their research. Although the typologies and numbers vary based on the researcher, I have identified six of the more common categories identified by a number of researchers: the criminal, the mentally ill, terrorists who are politically/religiously motivated, domestic violence, prisoners, or a combination (Blau, 1994; Butler, Leitenberg, & Fuselier, 1993; Herndon, 2009; Miller, 2007). Within the aforementioned categories, a negotiator will more than likely discover the motivation for the hostage taker's actions (Hammer, 2007; White, 1998). However, it is important to note that labels can be deceiving, and a negotiator must be open and flexible to the possibility that there is much more at play when he engages the hostage taker.

The cause of all critical incidents begins with an activating event triggering the incident. In many cases, the hostage taker may view the activating event as the last straw, meaning that the hostage taker can no longer cope or is overwhelmed; all coping mechanisms have failed (Veechi, Van Hasslet, & Romano, 2005). Beck (1999) describes the process of reaching a breaking point as a collision of one's personality and social environment, which creates a cluster of antisocial beliefs making the offender hypersensitive (p. 125). Beck describes these beliefs as rigid and uncompromising. They include the following: authorities seek to control me, and their actions are punitive; significant others manipulate and discard me; people outside of the trusted circle will hurt me; and paranoia (p. 127). The result is to strike back at what caused the pain, either imagined or real, be it an institution, person, or symbol. The inability to cope destroys the hostage taker's ability to think rationally and allows hostage takers to accept their irrational belief system. The negotiator must help the hostage taker identify the trigger and sort through those beliefs and feelings, and in perhaps full delusions, to resolve the incident. Two groups that present extreme challenges are terrorists and those who suffer from some form of mental disorder.

The Terrorist

Terrorists are very dangerous because their belief system is such that they are committed to a cause and if suicidal will become martyrs, seeing the hostages as only collateral damage, as in the case of Timothy McVeigh (Boltz, Dudonis, & Schultz 1996; Schlesinger & Miller, 2003). Although not a hostage taker, Faisal Shahzad, "the Time Square Bomber," made a statement to the court that exemplifies the terrorist belief system and indoctrination: "I want to plead guilty, and I'm going to plead guilty 100 times over . . . because until the hour the U.S. pulls its forces from Iraq and Afghanistan, and stops the drone strikes in Somalia and Yemen and in Pakistan, and stops the occupation of Muslim lands, and stops killing the Muslims, and stops reporting the Muslims to its government, we will be attacking United States, and I plead guilty to that" (Weiser, 2010, p. A 1).

The psychology of terrorists is further addressed in chapter 7.

Mentally Disordered

From a practical standpoint, it would likely be impossible for a negotiator to have an understanding of every psychological disorder within the American Psychiatric Association's *Diagnostic and Statistical Manual of Mental Disorders,* 4th ed. (*DSM–IV*). To compensate for this shortcoming, many agencies use mental health professionals as consultants during the negotiation process. Although agencies may utilize the services of a mental health professional, it does not negate the necessity of preparing for such incidents and understanding the complexities that certain disorders may present during the negotiation process. This section is not meant to be all-encompassing for every disorder, but to offer some insight into the more common issues that negotiators have faced.

To help negotiators appreciate the complexities that mental disorders present, Rodriguez and Franklin (1984) evaluated 86 hostage/barricaded gunman incidents faced by the New Orleans Police Department's Tactical Unit. In their analysis, it was determined that 66 percent of the incidents involved barricaded gunman, 27 percent involved hostage takers, and 2 percent were sniper incidents. They estimate that 60 to 80 percent of all critical incidents are caused by someone who is suffering from some form of emotional disturbance (p. 497). They noted that negotiators had problems in three areas when communicating with those who were suffering from a mental disorder: subjects who would not or could not communicate; psychotic subjects who were actively delusional or hallucinating; and subjects who were under the influence of drugs or alcohol. Each scenario created a level of frustration for the negotiator. To combat such frustration and foster a better understanding, the negotiators were later assigned to a psychiatric emergency room and performed intake interviews of patients who were identified as problematic in these ways. In a follow-up survey with the negotiators, it was determined that they had a better understanding of the most common populations that they encountered due to the psychiatric emergency room work, which reduced negotiator frustration and enhanced their negotiation skills (pp. 497–499).

There are several types of disorders that a negotiator may encounter, and they include schizophrenia, paranoia, depression, bipolar, antisocial, borderline, histrionic, narcissistic, avoidant-dependent, and organic brain disorder/dementia (Miller, 2007, pp. 68–80). James and Gilliland (2005) narrow the list to schizophrenia, depression, the inadequate personality (which is no longer recognized by the *DSM–IV*), antisocial, and borderline (pp. 451–454). Strentz (2006) offers the following general categories based on symptomatology of the categories overlapping: those who display psychotic behavior; those with personality disorders; and those who are in personal crises. It should be noted when one speaks of hostage takers that it is important to differentiate between juveniles and adults because of their maturity and psychological development (Strentz, 2006; Rodriguez & Franklin, 1984). From a negotiator's standpoint, I fear that if we attach labels to hostage takers, the negotiator will be forced to work within a box or will spend more time trying to diagnose the hostage taker rather than dealing with the issues at hand. Above all, it is important to note that the hostage taker's actions have created a critical incident and that within that incident a number of people are in crisis, beginning with the hostage taker and the hostages. The negotiator's job is to stabilize the situation and find a common ground from which the crisis can end peacefully. Herndon (2009) agrees with this observation, noting that the improper diagnosis of a hostage taker can cloud the negotiation process; more important than a diagnosis is the behavior of the hostage taker before and during the incident (p. 263).

There are a number of common personality traits that the negotiator will encounter: paranoia, delusions, hallucinations, disorganized behavior, jealousy, guilt, anger, rage, lack of impulse control, rigid thinking patterns and belief systems, suicidal ideations, and projection. Each of these personality traits is often compounded by the use of alcohol or drugs. When the hostage taker suffers from an existing disorder and uses drugs/alcohol to self-medicate, those substances become the catalyst giving the hostage taker courage to carry out an act. The motivations for such incidents, beyond the traditional criminal who gets caught in the act and the terrorist fighting for a greater cause, are many. Wilson (1993) offers insight into why people kill or commit suicide, and they are the very reasons why hostage takers take hostages: feelings of severe isolation, reaction to a situation that is no longer tolerable, hopelessness, the loss of a loved one through divorce/separation, history of passivity, and overwhelming feelings of hatred (pp. 107–109). In each of these cases, there is a sense of helplessness, a damaged self-image, and/or a loss of control either perceived or real. During this process, the negotiator should look to find a "hook," something that is special to the hostage taker, such as children, mother, or spouse. One word of caution: When a hostage taker rationalizes his actions by making a statement similar to "My mom will understand," this is an indication that the hostage taker is not afraid to commit suicide, or suicide by cop, and/or kill hostages.

CONCLUSION

The psychology of hostage negotiation is an acquired skill set that goes far beyond education. It must include training and application of skills. There are a number of variables that can and will influence the negotiation process, such as culture, mental status of the hostage taker, the use or abuse of drugs/alcohol, and the motivations of the hostage taker. The keys to a successful negotiation are adjusting to the needs of the offender; stabilizing the situation; and applying the skill sets of active listening, empathy, paraphrasing, and knowledge. The negotiator must find an emotional hook that has more meaning for the hostage taker than the crisis itself.

REFERENCES

Beck, A. T. (1999). *Prisoners of hate: The cognitive basis of anger, hostility and violence.* New York: HarperCollins Publishers.

Blau, T. (1994). *Psychological services for law enforcement.* New York: John Wiley & Sons.

Boltz, F., Dudonis, K. J., & Schultz, D. P. (1996). *The counter-terrorism handbook.* Boca Raton, FL: CRC Press.

Butler, W. M., Leitenberg, H., & Fuselier, G. D. (1993). The use of mental health professional consultants to police hostage negotiation teams. *Behavioral Sciences and the Law, 11,* 213–221.

Carmody, D. (1973, January 29). Brooklyn siege, for Murphy, was an ordeal of decisions; Frustration emphasized 'should we continue?' Shootout was an ordeal of decisions relief was difficult Murphy's 'first obligation' 'hostage training course' hostage release crucial. *New York Times,* p. 31.

Ensalaco, M. (2008). *Middle East terrorism: From Black September to September 11.* Philadelphia: University of Pennsylvania Press.

Farrell, C. (2010). *Terror at the Munich Olympics.* Edina, MN: ABDO Publishing.

Florida Department of Law Enforcement. (2008). *Florida basic recruit training program: Volume 1.* Tallahassee, FL: Author.

Gettys, V. S., & Elam, J. D. (1988). Identifying characteristics of hostage negotiators and using personality data to develop a selection model. In J. Reese & J. Horn (Eds.), *Police psychology: Operational assistance* (pp. 159–172). Washington, DC: Federal Bureau of Investigation.

Greenstone, J. L. (2007). The twenty-five most serious errors made by police hostage and crisis negotiators. *Journal of Police Crisis Negotiations, 7*(2), 107–116.

Hacker, F. J. (1976). *Crusaders, criminals, crazies: Terror and terrorism in our time.* New York: W. W. Norton Company.

Hammer, M. R. (2007). *Saving lives: The S.A.F.E. model for resolving hostage and crisis incidents.* Santa Barbara, CA: Praeger Security International.

Hammer, M. R., Van Zandt, C. R., & Rogan, R. G. (1994). Crisis/hostage negotiation profile. *FBI Law Enforcement Bulletin, 63*(3), 8–11.

Herndon, J. S. (2009). Crisis negotiation. In R. N. Kocsis (Ed.), *Applied criminal psychology: A guide forensic and behavioral sciences* (pp. 257–280). Springfield, IL: Charles C. Thomas.

Hogan, R. T. (1969). Development of an empathy scale. *Journal of Counseling Psychology, 33,* 307–316.

Hoppe, M. H. (2006). *Active listening: Improve your ability to listen and lead.* Greensboro, NC: Center for Creative Leadership.

Huber, D. L. (2006). *Leadership and nursing care management* (3rd ed.). Philadelphia, PA: Saunders/Elsevier.

Hunsicker, A. (2006). *Understanding international counter terrorism: A professional's guide to the operational art.* Boca Raton, FL: Universal Publishers.

Ivey, A. E., Ivey, M. B., & Zalaquett, C. P. (2010). *Intentional interviewing and counseling: Facilitating client development in a multicultural society* (7th ed.). Belmont, CA: Brooks/Cole.

James, R. K., & Gilliland, B. E. (2005). *Crisis intervention strategies.* Belmont, CA: Thomson Brooks/Cole.

Jones, J. (2000). *Modified F.I.R.E. model of crisis negotiation.* Gainesville, FL: Author.

Kanel, K. (2002). *A guide to crisis intervention* (2nd ed.). Belmont, CA: Wadsworth Publishing.

Kitaeff, J. (2011). *Forensic psychology.* Upper Saddle River, NJ: Prentice Hall.

Knudson, M. L. (1999). *Alachua County Crisis Center training manual.* Gainesville, FL: Alachua County Crisis Center.

Kulis, J. (1991). *Defining empathy and its role in hostage negotiations.* Chicago: Author.

Louden, R. J. (2004). Selection and training of police hostage negotiators: What's missing? *Law Enforcement Executive Forum, 4*(2), 47–54.

Louden, R. J. (2007). Local law enforcement hostage/crisis negotiation: An essay on continued viability in the aftermath of the attacks of 9/11. In O. Nikbay & S. Hancerli (Eds.), *Understanding and responding to the terrorism phenomenon: A multidimensional perspective* (pp. 167–179). Fairfax, VA: IOS Press.

McFadden, R. D. (1973, January 22). Robbers give up vow to die for 'victory and paradise'; 47-hour siege of Brooklyn sporting-goods store ends praise for police communication effort. *New York Times,* p. 1.

Mead, G. H. (1993). *Mind self, and society.* Chicago: University of Chicago Press.

Miller, L. (2007). Negotiating with the mentally disordered hostage taker: Guiding principles and practical strategies. *Journal of Police and Crisis negotiation, 7*(1), 63–83.

Passel, J., & Cohn, D. (2008). *Immigration to play lead role in future U.S. growth: U.S. population projections: 2005–2050.* Washington, DC: The Pew Research Center. Retrieved June 9, 2010, from http://mhsw.org/mental-health/immigration-to-play-lead-role-in-future-us-growth

Poolos, J. (2007). *Extreme careers: Hostage rescuers.* New York: The Rosen Publishing Group.

Regini, C. (2002). Crisis negotiation teams: Selection and training. *FBI Law Enforcement Bulletin, 71*(11), 1–5.

Rodriguez, G. J., & Franklin, D. (1984). Training hostage negotiators with psychiatric patients: A "hands-on" approach. In J. T. Reese & H. A. Goldstein (Eds.), *Psychological services for law enforcement* (pp. 497–499). Quantico, VA: Federal Bureau of Investigation.

Rogers, C. R. (1961). *On becoming a person.* Boston: Houghton Mifflin.

Schlesinger, L. B., & Miller, L. (2003). Learning to kill: Serial, contract, and terrorist murderers. In R. S. Moser & C. E. Franz (Ed.), *Shocking violence II: Violent disaster, war, and terrorism affecting our youth* (pp. 145–164). New York: Charles C. Thomas.

Slatkin, A. A. (2010). *Communication in crisis and hostage negotiation: Practical communication* (2nd ed). Springfield, IL: Charles C. Thomas.

Sonneborn, L. (2003). *Terrorist attacks: Murder at 1972 Olympics in Munich.* New York: Rosen Publishing.

Stamatis, D. H. (2002). *Foundations of excellent performance.* Boca Raton, FL: CRC Press.

Strentz, T. (2006). *Psychological aspects of crisis negotiation.* Boca Raton, FL: Taylor & Francis Group.

Terestre, D. J. (2005). How to start a crisis negotiation team. *Police: The Law Enforcement Officer Magazine,* 32–39.

Thomas, D. J. (2008). Culture and the hostage negotiation process. *Law Enforcement Executive Forum, 8*(6), 169–184.

Thomas, D. J. (2009). [Hostage negotiation and police recruits]. Unpublished raw data.

Veechi, G. M., Van Hasslet, V. B., & Romano, S. J. (2005). Crisis (hostage) negotiation: Current strategies and issues in high-risk conflict resolution. *Aggression and Violent Behavior, 10,* 533–551.

Volpe, M., Cambria, J. J., McGowan, H., & Honeyman, C. (2006). Negotiating the unknown. In A. K. Schneider & C. Honeyman (Eds.), *The negotiator's fieldbook: The desk reference for the experienced negotiator* (pp. 657–666). Washington, DC: American Bar Association.

Weiser, B. (2010, June 20). Guilty plea in Times Square bomb plot. *New York Times,* p. A 1.

White, J. R. (1998). *Terrorism: An introduction* (2nd ed.). Belmont, CA: West/ Wadsworth Publishing.

Wilson, A. V. (1993). *Homicide: The victim/offender connection.* Cincinnati, OH: Anderson Publishing.

Interview and Interrogation

INTRODUCTION

The goal of an arresting officer during a custodial interview is to obtain a confession. When a suspect confesses, they admit to the crime by confirming the known general details, as well as the details described as hidden crime facts. Hidden crime facts are those that have not been made public; the only people aware of them are police who have investigated the crime and the perpetrator. Much like hostage negotiation, obtaining a confession is an art that requires investigators to show empathy; play on the suspect's conscience, especially in violent crimes; know when a suspect is being untruthful; use trickery where needed; and possess the ability to move a suspect toward resolution and finding peace, if that is possible.

The methods used in obtaining a confession are governed by rules of law such as the Miranda decision, one of many laws that set the standard for interrogations. Although Miranda set the standard and the decision is now more than 40 years old, some police still have a problem adhering to this mandate. In this chapter, you will examine the Miranda decision and the laws that pertain to confessions, the differences between an interview versus an interrogation, the substance of an investigative interview, and the psychology of interviewing.

INTERVIEW VERSUS INTERROGATION

Since the Miranda decision in 1966, there has always been a differentiation between an interview and an interrogation. An interview is something that officers do to fact-find when they interview witnesses and victims. The interviews are structures with the intent of identifying certain facts like who, what, where, when, how, and why. Although Miranda is a landmark case, police in America have been known for heavy-handed tactics where suspects are beaten to obtain a confession. There are a number of court cases that address the abuse of people taken into custody for the purpose of interrogation. Consider two notable cases before the 1966 Miranda decision:

- *Brown v. Mississippi* (1936). The court stated that the use of force to obtain a confession makes the confession inadmissible.
- *Escobedo v. Illinois* (1964) guaranteed a defendant's right to counsel while in custody. Any information obtained after the request is inadmissible.

Even with precedents established by the Brown, Escobedo, and Miranda decisions, the public has been skeptical of police actions as they relate to interrogation, and this is especially true in the African American community. These views are not without merit. In area 2—a predominately African American community located on Chicago's South Side—the Chicago Police Department at one time routinely administered torture during interrogations. The methods of torture included electric shock, suffocation, and Russian roulette. The torture was investigated several times by the department, and nothing was done even after one investigation found the officers involved responsible for the acts (Ceon, 2006; Marin, 2004; Mills and Possley, 2005).

It is because of acts such as those, which were committed in Chicago from the 1970s until the late 1980s, that police are moving away from the term *interrogation* as it reinforces years of negativity associated with police and now with the war on terror (Crenshaw, Cullen, & Williamson, 2007; Palomiotto, 2004; Shuy, 1998). It is because of the images that are associated with the term *interrogation* that it has been replaced by two terms: *investigative interview* and *custodial interview.*

THE MIRANDA DECISION

The reading of Miranda rights when a suspect is taken into custody is the one thing that most Americans are familiar with regarding law enforcement practice, largely because the reading of Miranda was popularized with the 1960s television shows: *One Adam Twelve* and *Dragnet.* Although many believe that their Miranda rights must be read when one is placed under arrest, this is a misconception. The only time someone must be advised of their rights is when the person is in custody and police are preparing to ask questions about the crime for which they have been arrested (*Miranda v. Arizona,* 1966; Thomas, 2011). Another problem that arises with misunderstanding Miranda is inherent in the term *custody* and how the courts define it. Custody simply means that a person is under arrest and is not free to go. *Custody* and the concept of *free to go* can be interpreted differently by an attorney, suspect, and police, though. The final determination lies with the court and trial judge.

I have seen attorneys describe police intimidation tactics in obtaining confessions, after their client was asked to appear at a police station, in the following manner: "My client was asked to come to the station and did so on his/her own accord. However, when my client arrived at the police station, he was met at the front desk by an armed officer and had to be buzzed into the station by armed officers who stood guard at the front desk. Once behind the door, he was escorted deep into the station and buzzed through two secure doors where he arrived at an investigations area. He was escorted to a soundproof interview room by an armed detective. Once in the interview room, my client was scared and intimidated believing that he was under arrest, and that he had no choice but confess."

The attorney paints a picture of intimidation and fear, based on his client drawing conclusion from seeing what are necessary security measures of the department. Missing from the attorney's argument is one of two statements: "You are under arrest" or "You are in custody and not free to leave." If a person's freedom has not been taken away and they are free to leave, *Miranda* does not have to be read. If someone perceives, without verbal confirmation, that they cannot leave, that is not a problem for the police. Investigators don't tell people during interviews that they are free to leave, and there is no rule that compels an investigator to do so.

Even police still have a difficult time determining when Miranda applies, though. There have been a number of recent cases where investigators refused to honor a suspect's request for an attorney during a custodial interview. When a person being questioned requests an attorney to be present, the interview should stop until that attorney appears. Some investigators believe that the Miranda rules are meant or shaped to meet their needs, as in the case of John Couey who was arrested for the rape, live burial, and murder of Jessica Lunsford in 2005. In this case, Couey asked for an attorney several times, and his requests were denied. During the questioning, the detectives asked if Couey would take a polygraph. Couey responded by asking for an attorney. The investigator attempted to get Couey to be specific, asking if he wanted an attorney before proceeding with the polygraph, and Couey replied: "I want to talk to an attorney first" (Aguayo, 2006; Frank, 2006). The rules are clear; once someone asks for an attorney or even mentions the word *attorney* during a custodial interview, police must stop and confirm if the suspect wants an attorney. Failing to stop questioning and confirm if the suspect is making an actual request will result in any ensuing confession being suppressed, or thrown out of court. Below are two additional cases where investigators refused to comply with the standard set by Miranda in pursuit of justice.

- Greely, Colorado, April 2009: A judge suppressed the confession of a gang member and murderer of a transgender female. In the case, Allen Andrade arranged a date with Angie Zapata over the Internet. Upon meeting, Andrade inquired if Zapata was a man, and she replied that she was "all woman." Andrade grabbed Zapata's crotch and discovered a penis. Andrade beat Zapata to death with a fire extinguisher and robbed her. Thirty-nine minutes into the two-hour custodial interview, Andrade requested an attorney. The detective ignored the request, which resulted in the confession being thrown out (Dunn, 2009; Luning, 2009).
- Cape Cod, Massachusetts, June 2010: A judge suppressed the confession of murder suspect Julian Green. Green confessed in a letter to his girlfriend, to police, and to a grand jury that fired the gun that killed an 18-year-old man. Green was firing a gun along with another person in the street, and a bullet from Green's gun went through a window killing the man, Sellers. During his custodial interview, Green made the statement: "I think I need a lawyer." The investigator viewed Green's statement as a statement only and not a request for an attorney. In addition to the investigator's failure, the prosecutor failed to advise Green that he was entitled to an attorney during grand jury proceedings. The judge ruled that the confessions were tainted and suppressed them (Jeffrey, 2010).

When a person is in custody, meaning that they are not free to leave, they must be read their Miranda rights. And if they say *attorney*, the interview must stop, and the investigator must question whether the person is asking for an attorney. If so, no further questions can be asked until the attorney is present.

THE INVESTIGATIVE INTERVIEW

This investigative interview begins with a gruesome scenario that we will return to later. This was written to give you some material for thought and to introduce you to the complexities associated with an investigative interview.

Based on the evidence, you believe this is the suspect in that triple murder: What skills do you believe are necessary to obtain a conviction? A crime such as the one described in Scenario 6-1 is disgusting and will shock even a seasoned investigator. So how will you keep your personal bias from tainting the case? Will you be able to interrogate this suspect without becoming angry?

Interviewer Skills

In chapter 2, you were exposed to the many sides of the police personality. I describe what is known as a biphasic personality, which if successful, allows officers to compartmentalize certain aspects of their life. For some, it provides the ability to separate personal from professional. Based on the first half of this book, we understand that the ability to compartmentalize is difficult for police and that the job directly impacts their personal lives. There is no doubt that even the most seasoned investigator will have nightmares over such a crime scene, and to be effective, she must create a dissociative state of mind that allows her to depersonalize and detach from such incidents (American Psychiatric Association, 2000). Once the crime scene investigation has been completed, the investigator's focus changes from personal discomfort to becoming a spokesperson for the victims. An investigator's redirection of attention from the crime scene to a focus on the investigation serves two primary goals: catching the perpetrator of the crime and preventing future acts of violence.

To be successful during an interview process, an investigator must do homework, fact-find, and know all of the details of the case, especially those that are classified has hidden crime facts. Hidden crime facts are those facts known only to the perpetrator and the investigator. The sources of information in any investigation are witnesses, family members, friends, coworkers, and other associates. In addition to the facts, an investigator must understand human behavior, decipher body language, be deceptive if necessary, process possible motives, accept that a crime was committed "just because," and have the ability to establish a rapport with anyone. In many ways, the skills are the same for the seasoned interviewer and hostage negotiator: active listening, paraphrasing, the ability to minimize/use empathy, and knowledge (Schollum, 2005; Vandackumchery, 1999).

Another issue that police face when handling violent crime in minority communities of all kinds is the lack of participation or willingness to come forward as a witness or victim. That lack of involvement dates back hundreds of years. A more recent phenomenon associated with the hip-hop generation has been the Anti-Snitching Campaign publicized with DVDs, T-shirts, and baseball caps. Some supporters even wear those into the courtroom during trials (Asante, 2008; Hampson, 2006; Kitwana, 2003).

SCENARIO 6-1 TRIPLE HOMICIDE

Imagine you are the on-call homicide investigator and receive a call from dispatch at 2 A.M. directing you to the scene of a triple homicide. Upon your arrival, you meet with patrol officers, and they warn that the homicide scene is gruesome. They note that the only police activity in the house and around the exterior was to secure the crime scene and check for victims. Upon entering the living room, you discover the most horrific crime scene involving a family of three. You surmise that the following occurred, based on the evidence and a reconstruction of the crime scene: The suspect broke into the house through the back door, where you see fresh pry marks. Once in the house, the suspect entered the bedroom of the 13-year-old daughter, waking her with a weapon and forcing her into the living room, where she was tied to a chair and gagged. The suspect then entered the master bedroom repeating the same sequence of events, taking the dad first to reduce the threat, and then mom. Once all were bound and gagged, he beat the father while mother and daughter looked on. During this beating, he belittled the father attacking his masculinity and the fact that he was unable to protect his wife and daughter. The suspect then attacked the mother, torturing her in front of her daughter and husband, tearing her night gown and exposing her nude body. The mother was struck multiple times as evidenced by the bruises and abrasions covering her torso and face. The suspect tore off the mother's nipples. Apparently, the suspect used smelling salts to revive the mother so she could watch as he raped, tortured, and mutilated her daughter. Finally, the suspect returned to the angry, horrified father and cut his penis off while he was conscious, the last act of emasculation. He then stabbed the father multiple times. The suspect stabbed the mother, made a one-inch incision in her abdomen and placed her husband's penis inside the incision. He then cut the daughters throat and fled the scene.

   You have been unable to identify a suspect, and today, six months to the day later, an incident patrol catches a suspect attempting to break into a house at midnight. When the suspect is arrested, he has a bag containing duct tape, pliers, a hunting knife, and rope. A screw driver is also recovered. Currently, he is under arrest for attempted burglary, possession of burglary tools, and carrying a concealed weapon.

There are two factors that motivate people to join the Anti-Snitching Campaign: the reputation of police in minority communities for abuse of residents and/or the fear of retaliation from criminals if one chooses to co-operate with police. Although frustrating to the police and prosecutors, it is a way of life, often a survival technique for residents. Often, much of the information investigators receive in violent criminal acts comes by way of the family because someone on the street contacted the family or through an anonymous phone call.

The concept of uncooperative witnesses, victims, and suspects goes far beyond the minority community and fear of retaliation or mistrust of the police, though. There are other reasons for reluctance, which is termed witness/victim/suspect *resistance* during interviews. Those reasons can include embarrassment, inconvenience, loss of income, harming another, distrust and fear of the criminal justice system, refusal to take responsibility, trauma/fear of reliving the incident, self-disclosure, self-incrimination, loss of credibility with family/friends, and fear of reprisal (Schollum, 2005; Spencer and Stern, 2001).

Foster and Marshall (1994) understand the complexities of the interview process and the difficulties associated with remaining objective and unbiased. They note that an investigator must develop a mood of acceptance that incorporates the following: neutralizing personal moods; reading the other person's moods, be they a suspect, witness, or victim; and during the course of the interview, meeting the needs of each mood (p. 114). An interviewer is a facilitator and as such guides the interviewee over personal barriers to obtain details of the incident and support the forensic evidence.

THE PSYCHOLOGY OF INTERVIEWING

As stated earlier, there isn't much difference between a great police interviewer and a great hostage negotiator; both share much the same skills. The interviewer has one advantage in that in most cases the lines of communication are face-to-face, whereas the negotiator attempts to complete the task usually by phone. Face-to-face interaction allows interviewers to read and factor in gestures and nonverbal communication, which assist in the interpretation of the interviewee's emotions. Theories vary regarding how much we show through nonverbal communication, but gender and/or culture may make nonverbal communication a primary form of communication conveying a message as much as 50 to 90 percent of the time (Esposito, 2007; Kanu, 2009; Sethi & Adhikari, 2010). As we delve into the concepts associated with detecting deception, remember the discussion of nonverbal communication.

Detecting Deception

Police interviewers claim that they can tell when a subject is lying based on the subject's eye movement, posture, voice inflection, facial expressions, head position, and other actions. Researchers have conducted a number of studies in an attempt to determine if investigators possess this special ability based on training and experience, comparing the skill of the law enforcement officers to those of the general public in accurate conclusions drawn from such observations. In every study, there was no significant difference between accuracy of conclusions by police and the general public. The chance of accurate deception detection is little better than 53 percent, nearly even odds (Adelson, 2004; DePaulo and Morris, 2004; Wallace, 1999).

First, let's examine the nature of the research studies. Most, if not all, were performed in a sterile environment, meaning the test subjects viewed a 10-minute videotape to determine if a subject was being deceptive. But missing from this equation is the most important component—the interaction between the interviewer and the interviewee, which is essential in understanding the interview process and is a limitation in this study. The real keys to detecting deception are many: intimate knowledge of the case, information known before the interview such as lab reports and victim/witness statements, the setting of the interview, the nature of the interview (custodial or not), the interviewee's mood or attitude, the investigator(s) background/level of training/skill set, and the investigator(s) ability to establish a rapport.

Foster and Marshall (1994) state that no matter how hard one tries to appear under control, a person communicates subconsciously, and this behavior cannot be controlled. Subconscious behavior leaks into our surface behavior, our dialogue, and body language. Foster and Morgan note that no single behavior is a tell-tale sign of deception; however, they describe each subconscious utterance as a fumble, and when fumbles are numerous, they can be grouped together as a series of clusters classified as deception (pp. 65–66). Walters (2003) supports this argument and describes the leakage as being directly related to a human's fight-or-flight stress response, noting that the more stress an individual is under, the more difficult it becomes to censor nonverbal behavior or leakage (p. 109). Other indicators of verbal deception can be found in alterations of a subjects tone of voice, rate of speaking, change in pitch of voice, and volume, which all change subconsciously (Givens, 2008; Green, 2006).

In contrast is the argument that verbal cues present an interviewer with a host of problems. As mentioned earlier, the interview process and nonverbal cues are based on the concept that most people will do certain things when they are lying. As stated, it is impossible to hide nonverbal cues. This is demonstrated during a polygraph, as the polygraph measures baseline, starting physiological states, with a series of control (basic, non-emotion-evoking) questions, and then involves asking questions about the crime, tracking physiological responses and indicating when a person is being deceptive (U.S. Congress, Office of Technology and Assessment, 1983). The control is based on comparing relevant questions to nonrelevant questions and comparing the physiological responses. The controls established in a polygraph enable the polygrapher to make allowances for nervousness and body movement (Matte, 1996; Waid and Orne, 1981). However, one series of questions is not enough to supply firm conclusions. The same questions must be asked several times in different ways or wordings to establish that there is consistency in a subject's responses. Even with the controls in place, there are a number of false positives. It is questionable whether a human interviewer can possibly detect deception at the same level as a polygraph.

Vrij (2008) argues that the problem with police practices is that they have relied too much on nonverbal cues such as head and eye movement; posture; facial expressions; pupil responses; and arm, hand, and leg movements as the determining factors of deception, explaining that this is at odds with the results shown in the literature (p. 1323). Vrij would agree that the human ability to detect deception is a little better than chance. He attributes the failure to detect deception as a product of the reliance on nonverbal cues instead of analyzing verbal responses. There are other variables that have an impact on one's ability to detect deception, such as interviewer beliefs, type of interview—accusatory or fact-finding —and culture. Stockdale (1993) noted that other variables can influence the investigative interview; in most cases, police officers associated investigative interviewing with interviewing suspects, which presents a particular bias and hampers investigators' ability to fact-find (p. 15). If you were interviewed and during the interview were accused of committing a crime, and that line of questioning continued, do you expect that would increase your levels of discomfort and increase your stress response, which is directly associated with nonverbal cues?

Vrij, Mann, Kristen, and Fisher (2007) evaluated three styles of police interviewing—accusatory, information gathering, and behavioral analysis—determining that the best form of police interviewing is information gathering. In their findings, they note that information gathering produces the following: a greater number of verbal cues to assist in detecting deceit; a reduction in the use of physical cues in detecting deceit because of the many difficulties associated with developing such a skill set; and safeguards against false confessions and accusations of lying (p. 515). One observation several researchers have noted regarding accusatory interviews is that officers assume guilt and mendacity (untruthfulness) (Kassin, Appleby, & Perillo, 2010; Vrij et al., 2007).

If we dissect the research results in regard to the nature of police questioning, there is no doubt that there will be a certain degree of anxiety; however, the interview style may impact the outcomes and the assessment of the interviewee when it comes to nonverbal responses. If the questions are posed properly, as in fact-finding, it provides the interviewee with a platform to perform, and their words are the performance. This approach is much like an attorney questioning a witness when the attorney asks open-ended questions and then lets the witness hang themselves, so to speak, by offering too much information.

See Appendix A for an interview with the suspect described in Scenario 6-1.

If you examine the dialogue, the questions begin open-ended, providing the interviewee with an opportunity to explain his whereabouts on the night in question. With his own words, he leads us to his mother's house. I stopped the interview then, because everything from that point on depended on what the interviewee wanted to do, which could be confess, construct a story in an attempt to deceive regarding his involvement, or stop the interview and request an attorney. It is fair to say that as the questions begin to narrow in focus, the stress response will increase and there will probably be an increase in nonverbal deceptive cues.

Personality Types

From a tactical standpoint, I have always classified the personality types that police encounter on a daily basis as either cooperative, potentially uncooperative, and combative (Thomas, 1989). The logic associated with these classifications is based on the idea that officers begin with a tactical disadvantage, be it in interviews or face-to-face encounters, because the subjects that officers encounter have the knowledge of the crimes, who committed them, and if they are wanted for past crimes, which places officers at a disadvantage. When we speak of personality types in relation to interviewing, it is important to move beyond the tactical by describing the personality types, moods associated with each, and the filter/characteristics they present during an interview.

- **Personality Type: The Feeler, or Introverted Personality.** A feeler handles stress internally and seeks homeostasis, or balance, and can gain that stability through bargaining if necessary (Foster and Marshall, 1994; Walters, 2003). Walters (2003) notes that the feeler processes information based on internalized emotions or observations that can best be described as perceptions (p. 262).
- **Personality Type: The Analyzer, Extravert E Personality, or Logic-Dominant Personality.** This type may express a range of emotions, but unlike the feeler,

this type is very cognitive in her reasoning, dismissing emotion (Foster and Marshall, 1994; Walters, 2003). Foster and Marshall (1994) note that the analyzer is so rational that the only issues relevant to this type are those that are within reason and logical (p. 139).

- **Personality Type: The Driver or Active Extravert E.** This type is energetic and his behavior is outwardly demonstrative; the driver/active extrovert has to be in control, or the center of attention. Walters (2003) describes the driver as impulsive with the ability to change topics or thought patterns quickly, and when responding to stress, this type is more impulsive than ever (p. 270). This type's thinking pattern is to attack stressors, which can be described as anger.
- **Personality Type: The Elitist or Ego-Dominant Extravert.** This type perceives herself as gifted and above the common man with a degree of exclusivity. This personality type does not have a plan to fall back on and is not prepared if failure occurs. When stressed, this type's response is depression (Foster and Marshall, 1994; Walters, 2003).

In chapter 5, I refused to use personality types, opting to provide you with more general descriptions because typing can lead to tunnel vision. Although the personality types are useful in understanding how a suspect could think, it is essential that investigators not get locked into one personality type, remaining open to the fact that an interviewee may change based on their mood or their understanding of the gravity of a particular situation. The concept of the personality and its ability to adapt is debated by Inabu, Reid, Buckley, and Jayne (2005) where they assert that the personality is rigid and inflexible and not condition specific, and that attitude is what changes (p. 81). The logic of Inabu et al. flies in the face of traditional psychology, which offers that the personality is flexible and adjusts to the environment. The only time the personality becomes inflexible and rigid is when a personality disorder is present (American Psychiatric Association, 2000; Gray and Zide, 2008). Daubert (2007) asserts that the personality has the ability to modify its behavioral responses in relationship to the environment and is used in either escape and/or preservation (p. 5).

The process of the investigative interview is about preparation and understanding the suspect. Sun Tzu (n.d.) offers great insight into preparation: "If you know the enemy and know yourself, you need not fear the result of a hundred battles" (p. 13).

FALSE CONFESSIONS

Before we start this section, I know there is one question and probably one statement that you will make: "Why would anyone confess to something they didn't do? I would never confess to a crime that I did not commit."

From a practical standpoint, and all things being equal, most if not all of us would never admit to a crime that we did not commit. However, all things are not equal, and the interrogation process can be quite intimidating. Imagine being interviewed for hours on end, with no relief, exhausted, all you want to do is have the questioning stopped. Because you have held out so long, police start lying to you by making such statements as the following: "Your fingerprints were found at the crime scene." "There is a videotape of you walking toward the crime scene." "They have your DNA, and it is you. C'mon, confess; tell how you did it." "Your mom says you weren't home that night." With such statements, many of us might begin to doubt our own innocence.

The U.S. Supreme Court ruled in *Frazier v. Cupp* (1969) that police can use trickery and deception to obtain a confession. The limits include police making threats, which causes coercion, making any associated confession inadmissible.

One of the most famous cases where police obtained a false confession in this way was the Central Park jogger case in 1989. The New York City Police Department interrogated five black males, and during the interrogation, investigators began to give the suspects details of the crime. As time went on, the alleged suspects adopted the information, began to apparently believe it, and actually confessed to the brutal beating and rape of the jogger. They were convicted of the crime, yet there was no evidence to support the conviction. In essence, the investigators exhausted the suspects, provided them with the hidden crime facts, convinced suspects to accept the story as theirs, and they confessed. The videotaped confessions were used against them in court for convictions (Dwyer, 2002).

Again, it is important to maintain the integrity of the hidden crime facts and allow the suspect to describe the details of the crime completely of their own accord. Costanzo and Leo (2007) classify the alternate type of confession as authentic-coerced, meaning that after long, intense interrogation, a suspect is convinced that he or she committed the crime; at the suggestion of the interrogators, the suspect comes to believe that they temporarily blacked out or have repressed memories of the crime (p. 75).

EYEWITNESS TESTIMONY

When we speak of eyewitness testimony, we want to believe that a witness to a crime can describe what they saw in detail. It sounds rather simple. You see something and have to communicate that information to the police. Yet if this is so simple, why, if we ask 100 witnesses to an event what they saw, do their descriptions vary widely? Didn't they all witness the same event? Yes, however, what they witnessed is influenced by their perception. From an investigator's perspective, it is important to understand that each witness provides pieces of information, allowing investigators to piece together the puzzle of what actually happened (Brewer, Weber, & Semmler, 2007; Hardy & Heyes, 1999; Kapardis, 2003).

Malpass, Ross, Meissner, and Marcon (2009) note that there are several factors that influence eyewitnesses accounts, including perception, memory, cognition, and judgment (p. 18). In addition to what was witnessed, police themselves may have a profound influence on eyewitnesses, in ways including the use of suspect lineups or photo lineups. During a police lineup, investigators must be careful to create one that is not biased in any way. For example, it would be inappropriate to show a Polaroid photo of the suspect when all of the other photos are drivers license photos. The different presentation makes one picture stand out. Also, it is inappropriate for investigators to even suggest that the actual suspect is in the lineup, because this pressures the witness to pick someone even if the suspect is not present (Acker & Brody, 2004; McCann, Shindler, & Hammond, 2004).

When it comes to handling eyewitnesses and victims, an investigator ideally meets them at the crime scene or has them describe where they were in relationship to the incident, to be aware of their vantage point. In addition, investigators need to consider the impact that an incident has had on witnesses' psyches and how that may impact—perhaps reduce or skew—their ability to recall. Finally, an investigator should have an independent investigator present the lineup to victims/witnesses. This removes any potential future concern that the lead investigator influenced the identification.

CONCLUSION

The investigative interview is governed by a number of rules, but police still have problems with legal constraints associated with the Miranda decision. The research indicates that police believe obtaining the confession is the most critical aspect of an investigative interview, when in actuality it is information and fact-finding that are most vital. Although the jury is still out regarding an investigator's ability to detect deception, and the methods used, an interview provides the investigator with valuable information. However, the key to the best interviews is the ability to understand the suspect and meet that person's needs through empathy, active listening, and asking open-ended questions.

REFERENCES

Acker, J. R., & Brody, D. C. (2004). *Criminal procedure: A contemporary perspective.* Sudbury, MA: Jones & Bartlett.

Adelson, R. (2004). Detecting deception. *Monitor on Psychology, 35*(7), 70.

Aguayo, T. (2006, July 1). Confession barred because of request for lawyer. *New York Times,* archives.

American Psychiatric Association. (2000). *Diagnostic and statistical manual of mental disorders text revision* (4th ed.) Washington, DC: Author.

Asante, M. K. (2008). *It's bigger than hip-hop: The rise and fall of the hip-hop generation.* New York: St. Martin's Press.

Brewer, N., Weber, N., & Semmler, C. (2007). Eyewitness identification. In N. Brewer & K. D. Williams (Eds.), *Psychology and law: An empirical perspective* (pp. 177–221). New York: Guilford.

Brown v. Mississippi, 297 U.S. 278 (1936).

Ceon, J. (2006, May 20). Burge report to go public; Judge orders release of cop torture inquiry. *Chicago Tribune,* 12.

Costanzo, M., & Leo, R. A. (2007). Research and expert testimony on interrogations and confessions. In M. Costanzo, D. Krauss, & K. Pezdek (Eds.), *Expert psychological testimony for the courts* (pp. 69–98). Mahwah, NJ: Lawrence Erlbaum Associates.

Crenshaw, R., Cullen, S., &Williamson, T. (2007). *Human rights and policing* (2nd ed.). Leiden, the Netherlands: Koninklijke Brill NV.

Daubert, D. L. (2007). *Understanding personality disorders: An introduction.* Westport, CT: Praeger Publishing.

DePaulo, B. M., & Morris, W. L. (2004). Discerning lies from truths: behavioral cues to deception and the indirect pathway of intuition. In P. A. Granhag & L. A. Stromwall (Eds.), *The detection of deception in forensic contexts* (pp. 15–40). New York: Cambridge University Press.

Dunn, S. (2009, March 12). Andrade's murder confession thrown out. *Tribune,* archives.

Dwyer, J. (2002, October 20). Crimes, admitted but not committed; Confessing can seem easy after hours in a hard light. *New York Times,* archives.

Escobedo v. Illinois, 378 U.S. 478 (1964).

Esposito, A. (2007). *Fundamentals of verbal and nonverbal communication and the biometric issue.* Amsterdam, the Netherlands: IOS Press.

Foster, G. D., & Marshall, M. (1994). *How can I get through to you?* New York: Hyperion.

Frank, J. (2006, July 1). Couey's confession won't get to jurors. *St. Petersburg Times,* archives.

Frazier v. Cupp, 394 U.S. 731 (1969).

Givens, D. (2008). *Crime signals: How to spot a criminal before you become a victim.* New York: St. Martin's Press.

Gray, S. W., & Zide, M. R. (2008). *Psychopathology: A competency-based assessment model for social workers.* Belmont, CA: Thomson Higher Education.

Green, A. (2006). *Effective communication skills for public relations.* Philadelphia, PA: Kogan Page.

Hampson, R. (2006, April 29). Anti-snitching campaign riles police, prosecutors. *USA Today,* A1.

Hardy, M., & Heyes, S. (1999). *Beginning psychology* (5th ed.). New York: Oxford University Press.

Inabu, F. E., Reid, J. E., Buckley, J. P., & Jayne, B. C. (2005). *Essentials of the Reid interview technique criminal interrogation and confessions.* Sudbury, MA: Jones and Bartlett Publishers.

Jeffrey, K. (2010, June 30). Confessions inadmissible in Dennis trial. *Cape Cod Times,* archives.

Kanu, A. M. (2009). *Reflections in communication: An interdisciplinary approach.* Lanham, MD: University Press of America.

Kapardis, A. (2003). *Psychology and law: A critical introduction.* New York: Cambridge University Press.

Kassin, S. M., Appleby, S. C., & Perillo, J. T. (2010). Interviewing suspects: Practice, science, and future directions. *Legal and Criminological Psychology, 15,* 39–55.

Kitwana, B. (2003). *The hip hop generation: Young blacks and the crisis in African American culture.* New York: Basic Civitas Books.

Luning, E. (2009, March 13). Judge tosses confession, gang links in Greely transgender murder trial. *Colorado Independent,* archives.

Malpass, R. S., Ross, S. J., Meissner, A., & Marcon, J. L. (2009). The need for expert psychological testimony on eyewitness testimony. In B. L. Cutler (Ed.), *Expert testimony on the psychology of eyewitness testimony* (pp. 3–28). New York: Oxford University Press.

Marin, C. (2004, May 5). The implications of torture; From Iraq to Chicago, appalling acts regarding the mistreatment of prisoners are unfolding; Seeing torture, stopping torture. *Chicago Tribune, 27.*

Matte, J. A. (1996). *Forensic psychophysiology using the polygraph: Scientific truth verification-lie detection.* Williamsville, NY: J.A.M. Publications.

McCann, J. T., Shindler, K. L., & Hammond, T. R. (2004). The science and pseudoscience of expert testimony. In S. O. Lilienfeld, S. J. Lynn, J. M. Lohr, & C. Tavris (Eds.), *Science and pseudoscience in clinical psychology* (pp. 77–108). New York: Guilford.

Mills, S., & Possley, M. (2005, December 2). 3 Burge cops get immunity in torture case. *Chicago Tribune,* A1.

Miranda v. Arizona, 384, U.S. 436 (1966).

Palomiotto, M. (2004). *Criminal investigation* (3rd ed.). Lanham, MD: University Press of America.

Schollum, M. (2005). *Investigative interviewing: The literature.* Wellington, New Zealand: Office of the Commissioner of Police.

Sethi, A., & Adhikari, B. (2010). *Business communication.* New Delhi: Tata McGraw Hill.

Shuy, R. W. (1998). *The language of confession, interrogation, and deception.* Thousand Oaks, CA: Sage Publications.

Spencer, S., & Stern, B. (2001). *Reluctant witness.* Covent Garden, London: Institute for Public Policy Research.

Stocdale, J. E. (1993). *Management and supervision of police interviews.* London: Home Office Police Research Group.

Sun Tzu. (n.d.). *The art of war* (L. Giles, Trans). El Paso, TX: EL Paso Norte Press. (Original work published n.d.).

Thomas, D. J. (1989). *Defensive tactics manual.* Lansing: Michigan Office of Criminal Justice.

Thomas, D. J. (2011). *Professionalism in policing: An introduction.* Clifton Park, NY: Delmar/Cengage Publishing.

U.S. Congress, Office of Technology Assessment. (1983). *Scientific validity of polygraph testing: A research review and evaluation—a technical memorandum* (OTA-TM-H-15). Washington, DC: Author.

Vandackumchery, J. (1999). *Professional police-witness interviewing.* Daryaganj, New Delhi: APH Publishing Corporation.

Vrij, A. (2008). Nonverbal dominance versus verbal accuracy in lie detection: A plea to change police practice. *Criminal Justice and Behavior, 35*(10), 1323–1336.

Vrij , A., Mann, S., Kristen, S., & Fisher, R. P. (2007). Cues to deception and ability to detect lies as a function of police interview styles. *Law and Human Behavior, 31,* 499–518.

Waid, W. M., & Orne, M. T. (1981). Cognitive, social and personality processes in the physiological detection of deception. In L. Berkowitz (Ed.), *Advances in experimental psychology* (Vol. 14, pp. 61–108). New York: Academic Press.

Wallace, P. M. (1999). *The psychology of the internet.* New York: Cambridge University Press.

Walters, S. B. (2003). *Principles of Kinesic interview and interrogation* (2nd ed.). Boca Raton, FL: CRC Press.

The Psychology of Threat Assessment

INTRODUCTION

The term *threat assessment* is one that has been used by the Secret Service with the goal of identifying a threat to the president, foreign dignitaries, and members of government for the purpose of preventing an assassination attempt before an assassin or group has the opportunity to carry out such an attack. The president of the United States has the benefit of having the Secret Service to plan every aspect of a trip. Weeks before the president arrives for a speaking engagement, the Secret Service has sent an advance team to that location, where they interview every known threatening person in that city, and those determined to be a danger may be detained until the president is no longer in that area.

However, the terms *threat assessment* and *targeted violence* have become mainstream topics of discussion and were brought to the attention of the American public when distraught workers with the U.S. Postal Service launched workplace violence. The popular term *going postal* emerged and is now associated with mass murder in the workplace.

Targeted violence may include celebrity stalkers and murderers; acts of domestic violence; terrorism; and school shootings. Can police do anything to stop these attacks before they occur? This chapter will examine the psychology, law, and limitations that make it almost impossible to stop such acts of violence.

TARGETED VIOLENCE

Targeted violence is a term developed in 1992 by the Secret Service in the Exceptional Case Study Project (ECSP), which was an analysis of the behavior of individuals since 1949 who were successful or attempted the murder of government or otherwise prominent officials (Vossekuil, Fein, Reddy, Borum, & Modzeleski, 2002, p. 4). Ultimately, the ECSP defined targeted violence as any incident of violence where an attacker selects a target prior to committing the act of violence (p. 4). The term *targeted violence* can be applied to any act of violence where it can be proved that there was premeditation and planning.

Targeted violence is not limited to attacks against persons, although those are the most common. Such acts have also been carried out against corporations and businesses. Most notable are the attacks of the Earth Liberation Front (ELF), which attacked American car dealerships in the early 2000s, destroying large sport utility vehicles (Madigan, 2003). Other types of businesses that have been attacked are abortion clinics and companies using animals for experimentation. The attacks against businesses are usually ideologically based. They are acts of terrorism.

MOTIVATIONS

In chapter 8, there is a detailed discussion regarding motive, noting that motive is very difficult to prove because it requires understanding what the criminal was thinking at the time they committed the offense. During a police investigation, officers are responsible for answering six questions: who, what, where, when, how, and why. In solving many cases, officers can determine the who, what, where, when, and how. Of the six questions, "why" is the most difficult to answer. We often have very little insight into an offender's mind before the crime; therefore, investigators are challenged to construct a motive based on the evidence. But targeted violence is often an exception, because there is premeditation and planning, and the perpetrator aims to make a statement through his crime. The messages are either implied or delivered through some form of communication, and some of the clear motives include rejection; ideological differences (religious, political, and/or ethical/moral); desire to impress; paranoid, delusional, psychotic, or enraged thinking; power/control seeking; or personal reasons unique to the perpetrator. To get a better understanding of motives, we will examine motivations of terrorists, stalkers, and perpetrators of school massacres.

TERRORISM

What does a terrorist look like? Is a person of Middle Eastern, African American, or Asian descent most likely to be a terrorist? The reality is that it could be anyone. Examine the acts of two American military men: Major Nidal Malik Hasan, a psychiatrist in the U.S. Army and an American-born Muslim, and Timothy McVeigh, a Gulf War veteran who was awarded the Bronze Star.

- November 2009, Fort Hood—Major Nidal Malik Hasan was a U.S-born Muslim serving in the army. Hasan killed 13 and wounded 32. Was he planted by Al-Qaeda as a lone wolf where he was encouraged to enter the army and, once there, reach a position of power and then kill Americans? Did he alone experience an ideological shift since the United States was at war with Iraq? Or was there a steady decline in his mental health that led him to turn against his country and fellow soldiers? Based on Hasan's background, should he have been rejected as a candidate for military service because of his religious beliefs? Or should he have been profiled out with his ethnicity alone as the basis for excluding him from the military?

  1. McKinley and Dao (2009) note that there were several issues in Hasan's life that had an impact on his psyche. The first is that he began to have a conflict between his religious beliefs and the wars in Iraq and Afghanistan and was unable to reconcile these differences. While obtaining his master's degree, he presented a PowerPoint presentation in one of his classes entitled "Why the War on Terror is a War on Islam" (p. A1). He was so conflicted and attempted to get a discharge, but because the army paid for his education and he had needed skills with the Arabic language, he was told that attempts to get out of the army would probably be denied. In addition, he was harassed by other soldiers because of his ethnicity (p. A1).
  2. Hasan lost his parents, one in 1998 and another in 2001, and after that turned to Islam in the hope of coping with the loss, yet was incapable of doing so.
  3. Hasan was a psychiatrist assigned to Walter Reed Hospital. After counseling soldiers for five years, he became deeply concerned regarding the horrors of war and sought counseling himself. As a result of interaction with returning veterans, he began to openly oppose the war (p. A1).

- April 1995, Oklahoma City—Timothy McVeigh, an American white male and veteran of the U.S. Army, bombed the Alfred P. Murrah Building in Oklahoma City in an incident known now as the Oklahoma City bombing. Was Timothy McVeigh an Al-Qaeda sympathizer who looked to harm the United States after serving in the first Gulf War? Or was McVeigh part of a domestic terror organization such as the Ku Klux Klan? Was there an ideological shift in McVeigh's belief system after his involvement in the first Gulf War? Was McVeigh insanely angry over what he believed to be attacks by the federal government against organizations and argued the U.S. government had gone so far that the founding fathers would become "physically ill and call for an immediate revolution against the current government"? (Michael and Herbeck, 2001, p. 30)

1. Truman (2010) notes that McVeigh was angered over the assault by the FBI and ATF on Branch Davidians in Waco, Texas, where 70 Americans were killed. The Oklahoma City bombing occurred on April 19, 1995, the anniversary celebrated by domestic terrorists in the United States. During the bombing, McVeigh wore a T-shirt with these words of Thomas Paine: "The tree of liberty must be refreshed from time to time with the blood of patriots and tyrants" (p. 71).

2. Anniversary dates are important to terrorist organizations (Thomas, 2011) as they signal a celebration of victory or may identify when a government perpetrated some form of perceived aggression against the organization, its members, or their respective belief systems. Schrich (2005) details the significance of April 19, noting that it is recognized by militia groups within the United States as a special day. The events with that anniversary date are the Oklahoma City bombing; the FBI assault on the Branch Davidians in Waco, Texas; the federal government launching surveillance of Randy Weaver at Ruby Ridge; and an attack outlined in the Turner Diaries (p. 70).

The Typologies of Terrorism

There are usually no visible signs that someone is a terrorist. We must begin to look at the psychology and what truly motivates terrorists. Motivation is uniquely personal for each individual or group. Much like serial killers, there are a number of terrorist typologies; each is an attempt to best identify a group based on ideology or motivation. My experience across years shows that it is very difficult to create a typology that is universal for this group, because the landscape of extremism is ever-changing. Many of these groups dissolve and reformulate with a new agenda at will. Yet, I would be remiss if I did not present some of the more prominent theorists and their typologies before presenting a fairly simplistic set of typologies with clear distinctions.

Gurr (1989) offers four typologies of terrorism, which are based on the ideological beliefs or political affiliations of the group and its members: (1) Vigilante terrorism, which includes acts initiated by private groups toward private groups in opposition to social change. (2) Insurgent terrorism, which includes acts by private groups against public figures or institutions with the goal of forcing radical political change. (3) Transnational terrorism, which includes international incidents where the planning and training take place in one country and the attack occurs in another, such as the attacks in the United States on September 11. (4) State terrorism, which is the type of terrorism most closely associated with a government attacking its own citizens in an attempt to establish absolute control or quell political dissent, such as the South African apartheid and action in Nazi Germany (pp. 203–207).

Similar to Gurr's typologies are the typologies and classifications of Post (2007), who pegs terrorism into three primary categories—political, criminal, and pathological, with political terrorism being the most detailed and carrying a number of subcategories. The subcategories of political terrorism are what Post classifies as substate terrorism. Those categories of terrorism include: left wing, right wing, national separatist, religious, and single issue (p. 4). Other categories of political terrorism are state supported where countries train and fund acts of terrorism in other countries, similar to transnational terrorism, and regime or state terrorism, where the government utilizes its resource against its people to maintain power, also an aspect of Gurr's typologies (p. 4).

To simplify understanding of typologies, and the psychology associated with acts of terrorism, I will outline four general typologies based on ideological belief systems and motivations. The four typologies to be examined are: right wing, left wing, religious, and single issue.

Right-Wing Extremists/Terror Organizations

Right-wing terror organizations in the United States are associated with the Christian Identity Movement, with groups including the Arizona Patriots, Aryan Nations, Christian Defense League, the Covenant, the Sword, the Arm of the Lord (CSA), and the Ku Klux Klan. The ideology of these groups is the superiority of the white race, a disdain for lesbians and homosexuals, a hatred of the federal government and its agents, and distrust of mass media (Gurr, 1998; Laqueur, 1999; Smith, 1994; White, 2006). Laqueur (1999) notes that the groups are highly organized and often splinter, but their ideological teachings are a catalyst in the development of individual terrorists and/or small groups (p. 108).

The concept of smaller groups and a leaderless resistance was the idea of Louis Beam, who is described by the Anti-Defamation League (1996) as a sometimes Klansman, neo-Nazi, and leading advocate of antigovernment action (p. 6). In an essay written by Louis Beam in 1992 and published in the now defunct newsletter *The Seditionist,* Beam advocates leaderless resistance, noting that formal organizations and their structures are dangerous for participants in a resistance movement because they can be easily tracked and destroyed by the government (Anti-Defamation League, 1996, p. 7). Beam argues that a *cell system* is more efficient because cells are much smaller, there is an increase in unit cohesiveness, and there is limited likelihood of government infiltration and/or discovery. This concept has become the battle cry of Tom Metzger, the founder of the White Aryan Resistance (WAR), who supports the concept of the lone wolf in his teachings and writings. Metzger argues that the acts of Timothy McVeigh and those like him are examples of a lone wolf, and he claims them to be "our soldiers" (Seligman, 2001).

In addition to traditional right-wing terror groups, there has been a resurgence of modern-day militia groups, which are small town in their belief system and advocate home rule. They believe that any type of enforcement above the sheriff is unwarranted. Their strongholds are in Michigan and Montana. They fear big government, taxation, the loss of guns, and in general the loss of their freedom as Americans. Laqueur (1999) states: "America as these people see it, is ruled by Illuminati, Jews, Wall Street, the United Nations, the Trilateral Commission, and a variety of other groups, all aiming to subjugate and Balkanize the nation" (p. 110).

The threat of such groups is ever present, as proved by the raid and arrest of members of a Michigan Christian militia group known as the Hutaree when it was alleged that they planned to kill a law enforcement officer and then launch an attack at the officer's funeral (Bunkley, 2010). Group members, in essence, feel that the phrase "We the People" no longer has validity in this country, and that as citizens they have no control over their destiny. A similar sense of paranoia is evident in the Tea Party's rebellion of 2010, launched after President Obama started to implement his political agenda. Members of the Tea Party argue the same issues as volatile militia groups; however, they use the ballot as opposed to violence. Take a moment to reflect on these questions: Do the actions of the U.S. government warrant this type of armed response? Are militia groups a threat to the sovereignty of the United States? Do the actions of such groups as the Tea Party create an atmosphere that fosters a certain type of paranoia, or fanaticism, which can spur splinter groups that believe the only way to stop the government is through acts of violence?

Left-Wing Extremists/Terror Organizations

Left-wing terror organizations have a much different agenda than that of the right wing, with two goals—social revolution and/or separatism. Their ideological beliefs are based on Communism (George and Wilcox, 1996; Post, 2007; Purpura, 2007). They are in direct contradiction to right-wing extremists. However, both want extreme change in the current governmental establishment, and both advocate that their way of life and ideology is best for the United States. These groups were strong in the 1960s and 1970s, organizing students on college campuses to participate in protests against the Vietnam

War while demanding social change. It was the age of the hippie; the slogan of the day was "Make love not war." Some of the groups of the past were the Black Panther Party, Students for a Democratic Society, Revolutionary Communist Party, and the Communist Party USA.

Religious Extremists/Terror Organizations

Religion is one of the areas that may be central to a group's motivation and belief system. Extremist groups incorporate religion using God, or any deity, by arguing that this is not man's will but the word of God. By acting in the name of God, the group's actions are then just, and they will be vindicated. Reflect on the aforementioned argument of "God's will." Is it really God's will that right-wing extremist groups use violence as the vehicle for the United States to become a country for whites only? These groups use a religious saying to demonstrate that they are the chosen people, such as the Christian Defense League (CDL), which interprets John 3:16 to support their cause and ideology.

- John 3:16 actually reads: "For God so loved the world, he gave his only begotten Son that whoever shall believe in him should not perish, but have everlasting life" (Consolidated Book Publishers, 1968, p. 831). However, on the CDL Web site, they have interpreted the same passage as: "For God so loved the Adamic race that he gave his only begotten Son that any Adamite who believeth in him should not perish but have everlasting life" (Christian Defense League, 2010). The CDL manipulated the passage so their followers would believe that they are the direct decedents of Adam, the true children of God and white.

The same argument could be used when discussing the Qur'an, yet what is most known now about the Qur'an and its teachings is that Muslims have declared a jihad, or holy war, against the West and its allies. Depending on the scholar and the interpretation, *jihad* has many different meanings. Engineer (2005) argues that the term *jihad* is far from one-dimensional as viewed by the West and those who look to incite war. According to Engineer and other Islamic scholars, *jihad* literally means to make the utmost efforts, and the war is the fight within to controls one's desires (p. 126). However, in the world of extremism, *jihad* has come to mean "holy war." Kamrava (2005) supports this notion describing Islamic extremism as being divided into good versus evil, the oppressed versus the oppressor, the abode of Islam versus the abode of war—the best way to achieve their goals being the jihad, or holy war (p. 326). When we apply religion to extremism, it may best be stated that there is a certain degree of fanaticism and that the interpreter of the word can find an endorsement for nearly anything in the doctrines of the major religions (Laqueur, 1999).

Single-Issue Extremism/Terror Organizations

The focus of single-issue extremism is simpler to understand and follow, because for these terrorists, the cause is a special interest such as the environment, abortion law, or animal rights. Most of these groups have adopted the philosophy of a leaderless organization, as explained by Louis Beam and outlined in the discussion on right-wing terror organizations. Members of these groups have targeted abortion doctors and killed them, burned resorts or destroyed car dealerships that were deemed harmful to the environment, or destroyed labs where animals were being used to test cosmetics and/or drugs for which human testing is prohibited.

The Psychology of Terrorism

When you examine the typologies, it is inherent that each of the members and the groups has a belief system unique to that organization. There are many different types of believers, from those who are radicals to those who may be called sympathizers of the cause. Today, these groups use the Internet as a vehicle to entice newcomers, strengthen the bonds and beliefs of current followers, and solidify the conscience of those who are on the fringe by spreading propaganda.

Everyone who joins such an organization does not suffer from a mental disorder, and there is no evidence that there is a biological predisposition to join such groups. Research on the psychology of terrorism does not reveal predictable major psychopathologies and in fact shows that the most outstanding characteristic of terrorists is their normalcy (Goodin, 2006; Laqueur, 1999; McCauley, 2007; Post, 1998). So why does one become a terrorist? It is the collective group identity and the charisma of a leader, or if a group is leaderless, it is the literature, propaganda, and total package that a potential member finds enticing?

The goal is to transform one's individual belief system to that of the group. The danger of such a transformation is that the individual is incapable of thinking for herself.

Bion (as cited in Reich 1998) notes that there are three types of extremist groups based on their psychological needs: (1) the fight-flight group, which justifies its existence based on perceived threats; (2) the dependency group, which follows the direction of an influential leader; and (3) the paring group, which believes its acts will bring a new messiah (p. 32). Grossman (1995) describes the power of the group in times of war as the most powerful commitment; rather than self-preservation, the sense of accountability to fellow comrades becomes paramount. Grossman also explains that group actions allow for anonymity, as opposed to when an individual commits an act on his own and feels fully responsible for it (p. 149).

Grossman's observation is supported by Janis and his classic theory of groupthink. Janis (1972) offers that groups affected by groupthink ignore alternatives and make irrational decisions, which include dehumanizing other groups. What happens during the group dynamics is a process known in psychological circles as projection. In this case, the belief system/ideology allows the group to project every negative trait known upon its enemy. Dehumanizing the enemy allows terrorists to minimize the trauma or psychological impact of their actions. Timothy McVeigh described the children killed in the Oklahoma City bombing as "collateral damage" (Zinn, 2003). They were no longer human, not children, but damaged goods.

Groupthink furthers a cause and strengthens cohesion, and this creates the perception of injustice, the cry of almost every such group. Such thinking occurs in a vacuum and provides a skewed perception of reality. The symptoms of groupthink are an illusion of invulnerability, collective efforts to rationalize, belief in inherent morality, stereotyped views of enemy leaders, direct pressure, self-censorship of deviation, illusion of unanimity, and self-appointed mindguards (Janis, 1972, pp. 197–198). A final note regarding the importance of a group and acts of terrorism: often their actions are not about a cause, rather they are about the group, and their ideology rationalizes the acts of terrorism (Bergman, 2003; Martin, G., 2007; Post, 1998).

STALKING

Stalking existed long before it was criminalized. The lack of laws and a true definition were brought to the forefront with the murder of 22-year-old Rebecca Schaeffer, an actress who appeared on the television show *My Sister Sam*. Robert John Bardo, her attacker, had a history of severe mental illness. He was even described by one teacher as a "time bomb waiting to go off" (Douglas and Olshaker, 1998; Moffatt, 2000). Bardo became so obsessed with Schaeffer that on two separate occasions he traveled from Tucson to Los Angeles. On both trips, he was stopped by studio security and was unable to make contact with Schaeffer on the television set. So Bardo hired a private investigator to find out where she lived. When Schaeffer answered the door, Bardo shot and killed her. The tone of his obsession with Schaeffer had changed when Bardo saw her, on the television show, in bed with another actor. Bardo called her a whore, and insisted that God had appointed him as her punisher (Douglas and Olshaker, 1998; Moffatt, 2000).

After the murder of Schaeffer, California passed the first antistalking legislation. Although researchers have a difficult time defining stalking because of the various psychological components, and the statutes vary from state to state, three universal elements in the statutes say that one who:

1. Willfully, maliciously, and repeatedly followed, harassed or cyberstalked another and/or
2. Made a credible threat
3. With the intent to place the victim or victim's relative in reasonable fear of bodily injury is guilty of stalking (Florida State Statute 784.048(02)(3), Florida State Legislature, 2009; California Penal Code 646.9, California State Assembly, 2010).

Such acts are not limited to people with delusional obsession. The act of stalking may also be a by-product of relationships ending when one party is not willing to let the other go. When the stalker is not willing to release the victim, the victim is viewed as a form of property or at least subject to the stalker's power and control. Baum, Catalano, Rand, and Rose (2009) show in their analysis of more than 4,000 incidents that current and past lovers are most often perpetrators of stalking and harassment. Thirty percent of the victims were stalked by current or former intimate partners, and 22 percent were harassed by former or current intimate partners (p. 4). Consider these comments by stalkers that I have interviewed:

- "I love the bitch, she is mine."
- "If I can't have her, no one will."
- "He knows that I love him, so I don't know where he thinks he's going. I own his ass."
- "I guess I will have to kill her. She is only doing this to make me jealous."
- "I am not going to let anyone else have him, that's my man. I will kill the first bitch I see him with. I broke out the windows to his car and broke into his house and fucked up his furniture. Ain't no other bitch sitting on the furniture that we used. He needs to know that I will never let him go, so he might as well take me back because no one will love him like I do."
- "I took my shotgun and shot that goddamn sign because my girlfriend left me for her boss. I want them to be scared, and if I scare the shit out of her, she will come back."

With these statements, the suspect is claiming ownership of the victim. But on a more subtle note, what you should also detect is that there have been acts of violence in these relationships. In most cases, if there was physical violence during the relationship, that is an indicator that there will be acts of violence—harassment or stalking—once the relationship ends (Coleman,

1997; Hamel, 2006; Sheridan and Boon, 2002). Historically, the relationship has been fueled by an unhealthy attachment. An unhealthy attachment outside of any actual relationship may also exist, driven by obsessional fantasies like those of Robert John Bardo and his love interest in Rebecca Schaeffer, or John Hinckley Jr.'s attempted assassination of President Ronald Regan.

The Psychology of Stalking

Attachment theory was first presented by John Bowlby (1988), who defines attachment behavior as any behavior where a person seeks comfort in proximity from another who is perceived as able to cope with issues during times of extreme stress, fatigue, and illness (pp. 26–27). Bowlby is careful to note that when such an object of stability or comfort is removed, it becomes a stressor and creates separation anxiety (p. 29). A healthy solution for one who suffers from separation anxiety is to regain the sense of homeostasis by regaining the object of stability or accepting the loss and moving on. The alternative is rumination in regard to being abandoned, intense anger, threats, and ultimately acts of violence or harassment.

To expand Bowlby's research on parent-child attachment, Bartholomew (1990) applied Bowlby's research to adults and adult attachment. She described four styles of adult attachment in relationship to others: *Secure attachment* describes someone who is the by-product of warm and responsive parenting and as such is comfortable with intimacy and capable of autonomy within the relationship. *Preoccupied attachment* describes someone who experienced inconsistent parenting, which in response creates feelings of unworthiness, which explains a lack of love and attention on the part of parent. The resultant behaviors are deep-seated unworthiness and attention-seeking behavior to gain approval and love. *Fearful avoidance* describes a conflicted personality, one who desires social contact and intimacy but experiences distrust and fear that they will be rejected. To preclude these feelings, they avoid situations that would place them in harm's way. *Dismissing attachment* describes someone who believes that the only way to protect one's self-image from feelings of rejection and inadequacy messages from attachment figures is to develop a model of invincibility. Ultimately, these individuals bypass personal relationships and focus on activities like work and sports (pp. 163–165).

None of the aforementioned styles of attachment are permanent or static, a person may move from one category to the next depending on life circumstances and experiences at any given time. Fracturing or shifting of a positive self-image can be associated with trauma, the loss of a loved one, loss of a job, and other events that create self-doubt or an inability to cope.

Or the self-image may have never been developed, which was the case with both John Hinckley Jr. and Robert Bardo; both could be classified as having a preoccupied attachment.

Most of this discussion so far has focused on intimate partner violence. But in the study conducted by Baum et al. (2009), three other categories of stalkers and harassers were identified: *suspects who knew the victims,* which were co-workers, classmates, friends, relatives, neighbors, and acquaintances, accounted for 45 percent of the stalking victims and 44 percent of the harassment victims; *suspects who were strangers* accounted for 9 percent of the stalking victims and 12 percent of the harassment victims; and *suspects who were unknown* accounted for 15 percent of the stalking victims and 20 percent of the harassment victims (p. 4).

It is almost understandable when you think of an intimate partner breakup that there are some residual feelings of hurt, anger, entitlement, resentment, and in many cases a sense of loss, which coincides with the discussion of attachment. However, what is missing from the findings of Baum et al. (2009) is how or even why these other groups become involved in such behavior. After the death of Rebecca Schaeffer, there was a watershed of activity including the inception of the Threat Management Unit (TMU) by the Los Angeles Police Department (Boles, 2001; Martin, G., 2007). The first stalking article was published in 1993 by members of the TMU and their analysis of 74 cases. They originally identified three types of stalker/victim relationships and have since added a fourth: simple obsessional, love obsessional, erotomanic, and false victimization syndrome (Zona, Palarea, & Lane, 1998; Zona, Sharma, & Lane, 1993).

A simple obsessional relationship occurs when the suspect and victim have some prior knowledge of each other. This is similar to the Baum et al. (2009) category where suspects knew the victims or were involved romantically. The subcategories in this classification are as follows:

1. *Intimate* where domestic violence was perpetrated within the relationship. In this category, the stalker's motivation is to force the ex-partner back into a relationship or seek revenge by making the ex-partner's life unbearable (Baum et al., 2009 p. 76).
2. *Brief dating* is where there was no violence and one partner decided the relationship could continue (p. 77). In certain cases, the aggrieved party feels a loss of control and senses damage to his self-image, which directly corresponds to Bartholomew's (1990) preoccupied attachment. If a mental disorder exists, then the perception and anger are magnified exponentially with an exhibition of physical stalking and/or threats to do bodily harm.
3. *Nonintimate workplace* can best be described as present for those employees who have been suspended or terminated (p. 77). The employee targets a particular

supervisor or coworkers or any combination thereof for being responsible for her problem. The employee ruminates regarding his fellow workers until the outcome is an attack at the workplace. This is a *going postal* situation.

4. *Workplace adoration* is when one employee becomes infatuated with another employee as his advances have been rejected (p. 77). This rejection leads to anger and stalking.

5. *Non-intimate relationships* coincides with the Baum et al. (2009) category of suspects who knew their victims. The relationships include teachers/students, coworkers, physicians/patients, neighbors, roommates, and friends. Stalking occurs in these cases due to an actual or perceived wrong, or because the perpetrator's romantic advances were ignored. The victim may make a statement similar to "I don't want to ruin a perfect friendship by becoming romantic." The suspect may make statements similar to "You used me. See everything that I did for you, and this is how you treat me."

Love obsessional is the most dangerous. It is described as the lack of any form of relationship and meshes with the Baum et al. (2009) category of strangers and the unknown. The subcategories to this classification are as follows:

1. *Famous/public figure love obsessional* involves mostly stalkers who have never been involved in what can be described as a healthy relationship (p. 78). These behavioral clusters coincide with Bartholomew's (1990) description of preoccupied attachment. The perpetrator in these cases believes that if she were known to the victim, they could enter into an intimate relationship. The stalker begins a letter-writing campaign or may attempt to reach the victim by phone or e-mail. Oftentimes, they are ignored as was the case with John Hinckley Jr., or the love object does something to offend the perpetrator as was the case of Rebecca Schaeffer when Robert Bardo saw her in bed with another actor. Because of the failed advances or perceived wrongdoing, the suspect commits acts of violence.

2. *Ordinary/common citizen love obsessional* involves stalkers whose behavior begins when they obtain the victim's contact information through a number of possible sources such as overhearing the victim giving someone their telephone number or through social networks such as Twitter, Facebook, Flickr, and so forth. Baum et al. (2009) would categorize this perpetrator as a stranger or unknown. The campaign of stalking begins when the victim rejects the stalker, yet according to Zona et al. (1998) this category is far less dangerous than simple obsessional, primarily because the behavior is more about harassing than physical stalking (p. 78).

An erotomanic is an individual who has a delusional love interest. *The Diagnostic and Statistical Manual—Text Revised* (American Psychiatric Association, 2000) (*DSM–IV–TR*) explains that such a relationship is an idealized romantic or spiritual relationship, as opposed to a realistic romantic one

(p. 324). The victim is usually someone with a higher status such as an entertainer, politician, boss, teacher, doctor, or employer. The perpetrator will use any type of contact to get the victim to respond, even stalking. Zona et al. (1998) note that this group is very aggressive; however, such cases rarely result in any form of physical violence (p. 79).

False victimization syndrome is the final category of Zona et al. (1998) This group is unique in that the behavior is attention seeking, and the claims of stalking are false (p. 79). This offender generates false police reports, believing that if he can create an atmosphere where he seems to have become a victim with the potential of harm of violence, this will make his lover return. This personality type fits neatly into Bartholomew's (1990) preoccupied attachment theory.

The psychology of stalking makes clear that each of these individuals has a personality deficit, or there is a need that has not been fulfilled; as humans, we seek the pieces that make us whole, secure, and comfortable in our daily lives. In most of these instances, the perpetrators exhibit behavioral cues that may appear as a single cue or can be exhibited in tandem and that can indicate there is a psychological disorder: anger; fear; entitlement, depending on the nature of the relationship; rumination over some issue, be it a lost love or the inability to create a healthy bond or attachment; a damaged sense of self, which is offset by acting out with attention-seeking behavior; issues of power and control; jealousy; paranoia; hallucinations; disorganized cognitive processes; mood swings; and finally delusions in thinking. Based on the aforementioned behavioral symptoms, some of the disorders associated with stalking are histrionic personality disorder, narcissistic personality disorder, borderline personality disorder, schizophrenia, bipolar disorder, and delusional disorder and its two subtypes erotomanic and jealous type. This list is not all inclusive but drawn from the symptoms that each of the disorders displays.

A final note: The Internet and social networks have become a stalker's paradise. Many state that they could not live without Facebook, Craigslist, or Twitter, and this says as much about their personality needs as the stalker who is predatory and looking for the next victim. This atmosphere has created an unusual form of trust where victims have had their identity stolen, been harassed, and in some cases have lost their lives.

SCHOOL SHOOTINGS

School shootings are another form of terrorism, but the killers are juvenile and, according to the research, are retaliating much like an employee who feels that he has been wronged at his place of employment. Much has been said regarding the stress that juveniles endure. From an adult perspective, we ask the question, What stress? And we often respond by saying, "The only thing we ask our kids to do is go to school, stay out of trouble, and get good grades." However, what adults fail to recognize are the juvenile's relationships with teachers, peers, and their environment. Each has unique demands and requires the juvenile to adjust in order to fit in, or survive. How many different personalities do you exhibit? I am not asking whether you are like Sybil who had 13 personalities; what I am asking is whether there is a different you depending on the situation. Are you different with your friends than with your significant other? Is there a different you when you are in the role of parent? How about at work? All of these roles we play require different behavior.

Parents often dismiss the importance or recognition of youth relationships with peers and the pressure to conform. In addition, adults often forget how cruel juveniles can be to one another when it comes to appearance, clothing, body type, financial situation, and family problems. At the same time, a juvenile's hormones are raging, which has much to do with juvenile behavior and ability to cope. Thrown into this mix are idols that they identify with. So what are their coping skills, and how have they been taught to deal with stress? And what role do parents play in their child's problem-solving ability? To stop the attacks, either perceived or real, juveniles have resorted to violence by killing their classmates who bully and tease and school administrators who have failed to address the problem. And when they don't possess the ability to retaliate, they have resorted to suicide. It is only then that parents, school officials, and law enforcement understand the psychological torture a youth experienced.

Social Learning and Modeling

We are social beings and as such our personalities are defined through social learning, which begins at birth. Our personalities receive input from family, culture, and social interaction. It is through this process that we learn to accept or reject attitudes, belief systems, and behaviors.

Associated with the concept of social learning is the role of adults and, in some cases, peers who act as filters or govern what is acceptable through teaching and, where necessary, punishment. In essence, social learning is a process of trial and error with positive and negative reinforcements much like Skinner and Pavlov and their theories of operant and classical conditioning.

Bandura (1973) supports the idea that humans learn from observation and mimic what they learn. He also notes that observation teaches us the consequences of the new behavior, calling this vicarious reinforcement (p. 68).

Bandura divides the observational learning process into four components: attentional processes, retention processes, motor reproduction processes, and reinforcement and motivational processes (pp. 69–72).

Of the four components, the one that stands out most is reinforcement and motivational processes, because it is closely associated with reward and punishment. What we must understand is that juveniles are impressionable and choose their heroes out of adoration, popularity, and perceived power. When a hero possesses these characteristics, the juvenile will minimize the hero's criminal acts rationalizing their behavior. Without intervention or a reality check, this fantasy becomes the breeding ground for irrational cognitive processes and irrational problem solving. For the juvenile, a hero may be the local drug dealer, pimp, gang, rapper, athlete, video game villain/hero, or fictional character in a movie or television show. All have several things in common, most notably, success, perceived power, and wealth. Central to this theme is being cool, popular, and accepted. Although these are all outside the family unit, the impact of parenting and how parents themselves engage in their environment is also very powerful.

How this generation of juveniles learns and communicates is different than that of the baby boomers. In chapter 2, I discussed Generations X and Y; however, the group to be discussed here is the Millennial Generation, born 1981–1999. Lancaster and Stillman (2005) note that it is important to understand that technology and media have blurred the lines between fantasy and reality for the Millennial Generation (p. 28). Teenage Research Unlimited supports the assertions of Lancaster and Stillman, noting that today more than 80 percent of the teenagers have Internet access, whether at home, school, work, a friend's home, or the library. A recent study by the Fortino Group further predicts those between 10 and 17 years of age will spend one-third of their lives (23 years) on the Internet (The Kellogg School of Management, n.d.). In the realm of daily living, millennials' lives are influenced by technology first. Because they spend much of their time playing video games, texting instead of talking, and surfing the Internet, they have developed few problem-solving skills or the necessary filters if their parents are not involved.

The importance of parents acting as a filter, their child-rearing techniques, and how they view the world should not be underestimated. Kornadt (2002) supports this argument in his discussion of motivational theory, noting that differences in the child-rearing techniques of mothers are relevant to the aggressiveness or lack thereof in a child—most notably, how mothers dealt with their children during conflict, how mothers interpreted misbehavior, and if they approved of different forms of aggression (p. 193). Kornadt states that there is a circle of interaction within the family that establishes attitudes, expectations, reactions, and effects that create the platform for motives and the personality for years (p. 197). Other factors that have an impact on a juvenile's development of motives are interactions with fathers, extended family, peer groups, school, and the environment (p. 197).

The Psychology of School Shootings

The theme of this chapter has focused on juveniles' inability to manage their anger properly. However, from a layman's view, you have to wonder why the kids who have perpetrated school massacres are so angry. And what is the source of their anger? In 2002, researchers Vossekuil et al. examined school shootings under the auspices of the U.S. Secret Service and the U.S. Department of Education in an attempt to understand these phenomena. Vossekuil et al. examined 37 incidents committed by 41 individuals from December 1974 through May 2000. The sources of data collection were investigative, school, court, and metal health records. In addition to these records, the researchers interviewed 10 of the perpetrators, which gave the researchers an opportunity to understand the attackers from inception to attack (pp. 8–9).

Vossekuil et al. (2002) determined that 71 percent of the attackers felt threatened, persecuted, bullied, attacked, or injured by classmates. The bullying and harassment was something the attackers experienced for a length of time and was described as severe. Fellow students also described many of the attackers as people everyone liked to tease (Leburn, 2009). If you examine this information alone, it means that the attackers' image of self had been destroyed, there was a sense of hopelessness, and there was no relief. In addition to the personal attacks, most of the attackers (98%) had difficulty coping with losses either perceived or actual, which included loss of status, loss of a loved one, loss of a romantic relationship, or a major illness experienced by themselves or someone to whom they were close. As a result, many of the attackers either considered or attempted suicide (p. 23).

Beck (1999) argues that due to an interaction between one's environment and personality, the individual may develop what he describes as a cluster of antisocial concepts and beliefs, which reflect the offender's personal vulnerability (p. 125). The actions of others are viewed as antagonistic, controlling, and damaging to the offender's image of self. In order regain control, the offender must become the aggressor, viewing it as a way to maintain freedom, gain the respect of others, and stop future attacks. Beck notes that when an attacker is primed to strike back, he has rationalized his actions by making them personal, only recognizing that which supports his belief system and viewing the intentions of others as manipulative. He refuses to take responsibility for his actions, rationalizing that it is the action of others that created this situation (p. 127).

If we examine the discussions of Vossekuil et al. (2002) and Beck (1999), the attackers are unable to cope with a number of issues, or they become overwhelmed, perceive they have no control, and look to strike back at the source of the pain. This type of skewed logic is not limited to perpetrators of school violence but is central to the entire chapter. And just as there is no profile of a terrorist or stalker, there is no profile of the perpetrator of violent school attacks. The recurring theme is rumination or the inability to process information cognitively to move forward. The concept of rumination is very important because the research shows that school massacres do not occur spontaneously but are well planned events with the attackers targeting their tormentors (Borum and Verhaggen, 2006; Leburn 2009; Newman, 2004). See Diagram 7-1, which summarizes the anatomy of a school shooting.

THREAT ASSESSMENT

Threat assessment is the ability to predict acts of future targeted violence, harassment, or cyberattacks against a particular target, be it an individual or an institution, during a specified time frame or window of opportunity. Some examples are dignitaries during their scheduled travels, governmental or educational institutions, employers or employees, family members, lovers or ex-lovers, celebrities, and so forth. Fein, Vossekuil, and Holden (1995) note that there are three functions of a threat-assessment program: identifying the perpetrator, assessing the risk of violence at a particular time, and managing the perpetrator and the threat the perpetrator poses to the target (p. 3).

Prediction

Attempting to predict future acts of human behavior is one of the most difficult tasks that a mental health professional or law enforcement officer has to face. Rice and Harris (1995) assert that in the case of predicting violence, it is well documented that mental health professionals possess no special expertise in the prediction of violence, and that reliance on clinical judgments alone results in numerous inaccurate predictions of violence and recidivism (p. 737).

From a mental health perspective, there are psychological instruments that are designed to assist the mental health professional, yet they have their pitfalls. Many are designed to be utilized without the subject in question being interviewed, relying on historical data with the understanding that the best predictor of future behavior is past behavior. Another pitfall is when the population used to obtain the data is skewed. Predictions based on the

The attacker has been bullied, ostracized, and considered an outcast by fellow classmates through middle and high school years

The attacker ruminates, and the feelings change from frustration to anger. The attacker blames his tormentors and school administrators for failing to intervene.

The attacker feels that he has lost control and needs to restore a sense of self and the respect of his peers. He studies the acts of other school attackers and episodes of violence to develop a plan of attack.

The attacker journals, writes poems, draws, and even blogs about his violent fantasies. Here he finds support for his ideas and has the ability to reinforce his skewed logic.

If there is no intervention, the suspect carries out his attack. If he does not commit suicide, he feels that he has been vindicated and gained the respect of others. In essence, there is a return to homeostasis.

Diagram 7-1: The Anatomy of a School Shooting

instrument might be questionable if it was only tested in a forensic setting such as a prison or mental health facility where there are certain controls as opposed to a population that is functioning in society where the social controls are much different and free will is ever present. The results may be adversely influenced by culture and ethnicity, which all instruments should address in order to be considered valid.

When attempting to predict behavior, there are four possible outcomes: false positive, false negative, true positive, and true negative. Watkins, Glutting, and Youngstrom (2005) note that there are only two correct outcomes: true positive and true negative (p. 256). In the case of predicting future acts of violence, a true positive indicates that the instrument correctly identified those who will perpetrate future acts of violence, and a true negative correctly identifies those who will not perpetrate future acts of violence. Meloy (2000) notes that there are two technical problems in assessing the risk of violence: false positives and false negatives (p. 5).

Meloy (2000) identifies three components of a base rate when predicting behavior: behavior, a group of people, and time frame (p. 5). If we go back and examine my definition of threat assessment, the same components are central to the definition. False negatives are a prediction by a clinician, police officer, or probation officer that a subject is not violent based on all of the relevant information, yet when released, they carry out an act of violence contrary to the prediction (Meloy, 2000; Watkins et al., 2005). Therefore, an assessor will probably predict that there will be violence when there will not, which is a false positive; Meloy notes that this will occur approximately 40 percent of the time (p. 11). The good news is that false positives prevent the potential tragic outcomes described in the false negatives. Finally, in regard to prediction and the use of psychological instruments, they are specific to the crime that they are assessing.

The Law as It Relates to Threat Assessment

From a police perspective, the law is very clear: for police to act there must be a clear violation of the law that meets the following criteria:

1. The criminal act in question encompasses all of the elements of the crime. This is important because if one element is missing, it may mean the difference between an immediate arrest, attempting to obtain a warrant at a later date, or dismissal of the charges. A simple example is the difference in stalking, a misdemeanor, and aggravated stalking, a felony, as described in Florida State Statute 784.048 (Florida State Legislature, 2009).

    a. The elements of stalking are willfully, maliciously, and repeatedly follows, harasses, cyberstalks another person; the perpetrator meeting these criteria commits the offense of stalking, a misdemeanor (Florida State Statute 748.048 (2)).

b. The elements of aggravated stalking are willfully, maliciously, and repeatedly follows, harasses, cyberstalks another person and makes a credible threat with the intent to place that person in reasonable fear of death or bodily injury of the person, or the person's child, sibling, spouse, parent, or dependent; the perpetrator meeting these criteria commits the offense of aggravated stalking, a felony (Florida State Statute 748.048 (3)).

c. The difference in the statutes is subtle but significant. The primary difference in felony and misdemeanor stalking is the credible threat and that the victim is in fear that the perpetrator has the ability to kill or seriously injure the victim or a concerned party.

2. If a criminal act is a misdemeanor exception or felony, it allows for immediate arrest. In every state, an officer can make an immediate arrest for a felony if they have probable cause to believe that the felony was committed and the perpetrator is the one who committed the crime. However, the rule of law is not the same for misdemeanors. They have two different classifications: (a) simple misdemeanors require an officer to complete his investigation and submit the investigation and complaint to the state attorney or prosecutor's office, and (b) misdemeanor exception allows an officer to make an arrest with the same standard of probable cause as a felony.

Another tool for law enforcement is civil commitment of subjects who suffer from a mental illness, and if it is determined that they are a threat to themselves or others or are unable to provide for their basic needs such as health and safety, an officer can take them into custody to be evaluated (Oregon State Statute 426.005, Oregon State Legislature, 2009; Florida State Statute 394.463, Florida State Legislature, 2009). This type of commitment is involuntary and not an arrest, but the sole purpose is a mental status examination, which is performed at a local mental health facility as defined by statute or the community. Finally, depending on the state, the subject can be held anywhere from 72 hours to 10 days.

For mental health professionals, the standard is similar if we are describing an involuntary commitment. However, there are court-ordered evaluations designed to determine if a subject is a threat. In these cases, the clinician acts in the capacity of an expert witness. During the court-ordered evaluation, the evaluator must look at the subject's past to include mental health and medical records; criminal history, paying particular attention to arrests for acts of violence; prison records if the subject has been incarcerated, paying attention to acts of violence; and family history, making sure to interview family members when possible, which should give a complete history of the subject and her interaction within the environment. If there is a victim who has been threatened, the evaluator must interview the victim to determine the nature of the relationship, if any, and the nature of the threats. Finally, after detailing the subject's history, the evaluator must administer the appropriate psychological instrument and interview the subject. Based on all of the data, then and only then is a clinician able to present their findings to the court with the understanding that there will probably be a false positive finding of approximately 40 percent, which is to err on the side of safety.

Mental health professionals also have a duty to warn if during their practice, it is determined that a client intends to harm another person. This was born out of a 1976 civil case known as *Tarasoff v. the Regents of the University of California.* In this case, a client confided to his psychologist the intent to kill Tarasoff two months prior to the incident. The psychologist had the client stopped by the university police to determine during a brief interview that his client appeared to be rational and had him released. The court recognized that there are limitations to one's ability to predict acts of future violence, but the therapist is held to the standard of at least warning the victim (therapist/patient confidentiality does not apply in these situations). The importance of the Tarasoff case cannot be overstated. In 1966 Charles Whitman advised a University of Texas psychiatrist that he felt like shooting people from the clock tower. The psychiatrist dismissed Whitman's statements, noting that they were commonly made by students. The end result was that he murdered 18 and wounded 31 (Levin and Fox, 1999; Nicoletti, Spencer-Thomas, & Bollinger, 2010). In some states, the duty to warn has been extended to law enforcement or the courts where they are required to contact potential victims when a perpetrator is going to be released from jail.

Threat Assessment Questions

Relevant to any threat assessment are the investigator's questions. In every criminal investigation, law enforcement looks to answer six basic questions: who, what where, when, how, and why. Although the answers to these questions are important, Fein and Vossekuil (1998) developed a series of questions that are essential in assessing a threat in regard to targeted violence and should be a starting point in a threat assessment.

- What motivated the subject to make the statement or take the action that caused him or her to come to attention (p. 55)? In the assessment of stalking, intimate partner violence, or a school setting, oftentimes the subject will be known. What needs to be addressed here is what the basis is for the behavior, and more importantly, why the subject is acting this way.
- What, if anything, has the subject communicated to someone else (target, law enforcement, family, friends, colleagues, associates) or written in a diary or journal concerning his or her intentions (p. 55)? In many instances—such as was

the case in the incidents concerning Tarasoff, Robert Bardo, John Hinckley, and Columbine—communication will give you insight into motive, the subject's cognitive processes, and their motives.

- Has the subject shown an interest in targeted violence, perpetrators of targeted violence, weapons, extremist groups, violent video games, violent movies, or murder (p. 55)? This is relational to the concept of groupthink and seeking to solidify a given perspective or position as Beck (1999) describes. The subject views the actions of others as antagonistic, controlling, and damaging to the offender's image of self.
- Is there evidence that the subject has engaged in menacing, harassing, and/or stalking-type behaviors? Has the subject engaged in attack-related behaviors (p. 55)? These behaviors indicate that the subject may be preparing a plan of attack. Because they are repetitive in nature, the subject is looking for weaknesses in the target's daily routine and security, as well as testing the target. With each repeated visit, they gain a sense of confidence much like rehearsing the event before the grand performance. Ultimately, the predator is preparing for the hunt.
- Does the subject have a history of mental illness involving command hallucinations, delusional ideas, feelings of persecution, and so forth, with indications that the subject has acted on those beliefs?

In cases such as this, the subject will probably be on some form of medication. However, many who suffer from mental illness don't like the way the medication makes them feel and refuse to take it. They view themselves as mentally competent, and it is the rest of the world that has problems. As was the case of Russell Eugene Weston Jr. who entered the U.S. Capitol building in July 1998 armed, killing two Capitol police officers. Weston suffered from paranoid schizophrenia and had been interviewed by the Secret Service and not deemed a threat (Grunwald and Boodman, 1998).

- How organized is the subject? Does the subject have the ability to plan and execute a violent action against a target (p. 56)?
- Is there evidence that the subject is experiencing desperation and/or despair? Has the subject experienced a recent personal loss and/or loss of status? Is the subject now, or has the subject ever been, suicidal (p. 56)? The central themes of this chapter have been about a wrong, whether real or imagined; a damaged self or ego; anger; and the inability to cope.
- Is the subject's story consistent with her actions?
- Are those who know the subject concerned that he or she might take action based on inappropriate ideas?
- What factors in the subject's life and/or environment might increase or decrease the likelihood that the subject will attempt to attack a target (or targets)?

CONCLUSION

When discussing the psychology of threat assessment, it is undoubtedly one of the most difficult tasks an assessor has to complete. We know that the assessor doesn't possess a crystal ball and that they have to rely on interviews and case histories to predict acts of future violence. Looming in the ability to predict is a certain degree of uncertainty and the knowledge that if the assessor makes the wrong decision, the victim could die. The case of Eugene Weston Jr., the U.S. Capitol shooter, emphasizes the difficulty of assessing a threat in regard to acts of future violence. Here is the dilemma faced by all assessors: What happens if they deem someone a threat? There are limitations, but the subject can be managed by court order, treatment, and monitoring by the court, law enforcement agencies, as well as the mental health provider if the subject has broken a law such as stalking. If there is no criminal act, and if the subject meets criteria for involuntary admission, then that is an alternative; however, this is a temporary fix.

To complicate this matter even further, when we speak of terrorism, we may be able to identify a group or an individual if they have done something that has come to the attention of authorities. If they are acting in the capacity of a lone wolf or have become part of the leaderless resistance, we may never know that a particular threat exists until after the attack, as in the case of Timothy McVeigh. In fact, when hunting for these actors, it is like searching for a needle in a haystack.

The third group in question is school shooters. This group is probably the one where we have the greatest potential to intervene because the kids interact with the school environment daily, which includes teachers, peers, administrators, and law enforcement/security personnel. Based on the data, we know that this juveniles in this group have experienced a loss of some sort and don't fit in socially, and because of this, they are targeted by other students. In the case of Columbine, Harris and Klebold journaled, made a movie as a class project where they acted out the shooting of fellow classmates, and even wrote papers for classes that detailed acts of murder (Carducci, 2009; Gallimore, 2004). These warning signs were ignored, and the end result was the Columbine massacre.

If we examine the psychology of each group, it becomes apparent that these individuals suffer from unresolved anger and are unable to rationally resolve issues. In fact, in most of these cases, they feel so slighted that the only way to resolve the matter is through acts of violence. The unresolved anger, rumination, rationalizing the future acts of violence, and dehumanizing the victims becomes the catalyst for the ultimate acts of violence. If carried out, the act of violence reestablishes the perpetrator's sense of self and importance.

REFERENCES

American Psychiatric Association. (2000). *Diagnostic and statistical manual—text revised* (4th ed.). Arlington, VA: Author.

Anti-Defamation League. (1996). *Danger: Extremism the major vehicles and voices on America's far-right fringe.* New York: Author.

Bandura, A. (1973). *Aggression a social learning analysis.* Englewood Cliffs, NJ: Prentice-Hall.

Bartholomew, K. (1990). Avoidance of intimacy: An attachment perspective. *Journal of Social and Personal Relationships, 7,* 147–178.

Baum, K., Catalano, S., Rand, M., & Rose, K. (2009). *National victimization survey: Stalking victimization in the United States.* Washington, DC: Bureau of Justice Statistics.

Beck, A. T. (1999). *Prisoners of hate: The cognitive basis of anger, hostility, and violence.* New York: HarperCollins Publishers.

Bergman, W. (2003). Pogroms. In W. Heitmeyer & J. Hagan (Eds.), *International handbook of violence research* (pp. 351–368). Dordrecht, the Netherlands: Kluwer Academic Press.

Boles, G. S. (2001). Developing a model approach to confronting the problem of stalking: Establishing a threat management unit. In J. A. Davis (Ed.), *Stalking problems and victim protection: Prevention, intervention, threat assessment, and case management* (pp. 337–350). Boca Raton, FL: CRC Press.

Borum, R., & Verhaggen, D. (2006). *Assessing and managing violence risk in juveniles.* New York: Guilford Press.

Bowlby, J. (1988). *A secure base: Parent-child attachment and healthy human development.* New York: Basic Books.

Bunkley, N. (2010, May 4). Militia members released until trial in Michigan plot. *New York Times,* p. 16.

California State Assembly. (2010). *California Penal Code 646.9: Stalking.* Sacramento, CA: Author.

Carducci, B. (2009). *The psychology of personality* (2nd ed.) Malden, MA: Wiley-Blackwell.

Christian Defense League. (2010). *Creed of the new Christian crusade church: John 3:16.* Retrieved May 18, 2010, from http://cdlreport.com/

Coleman, J. R. (1997). Stalking behavior and the cycle of domestic violence. *Journal of Interpersonal Violence, 12,* 420–432.

Consolidated Book Publishers. (1968). *The Holy Bible clarified edition: The complete text of the authorized King James version.* Chicago, IL: Author.

Crain, W. (1992). *Theories of development: Concepts and applications* (3rd ed.). Englewood Cliffs, NJ: Prentice-Hall.

Douglas, J. E., & Olshaker, M. (1998). *Obsession.* New York: Simon and Schuster.

Engineer, A. A. (2005). *On developing theology of peace in Islam.* New Delhi: Sterling Publishers Private Limited.

Fein, R. A., Vossekuil, B., & Holden, G. A. (1995). *Threat assessment: An approach to prevent targeted violence.* Washington, DC: National Institute of Justice.

Fein, R. A. & Vossekuil, B. (1998). *Protective intelligence and threat assessment investigations: A guide for state and local law enforcement officials.* Washington, DC: National Institute of Justice.

Florida State Legislature. (2009). *Florida State Statute 784.048): Aggravated Stalking.* Tallahassee, FL: Author.

Florida State Legislature. (2009). *Florida State Statute 394.463: Involuntary commitment.* Tallahassee, FL: Author.

Gallimore, T. (2004). Unresolved trauma: Fuel for the cycle of violence and terrorism. In C. E. Stout (Ed.), *Psychology of terrorism: Coping with the continuing threat* (pp. 67–94). Westport, CT: Praeger Publishing.

George, J., & Wilcox, L. (1996). *American extremism: Militias, supremacists, klansmen, communists, & others.* Amherst, NY: Prometheus Books.

Goodin, R. E. (2006). *What's wrong with terrorism?* Cambridge, UK: Polity Publishing.

Grunwald, M., & Boodman, S. G. (1998, July 28). Weston case fell through the cracks. *Washington Post,* p. A01.

Grossman, D. (1995). *On killing: The psychological cost of learning to kill in war and society.* Boston: Little, Brown & Company.

Gurr, T. R. (1989). Protest and rebellion in the 1960s: The United States in world perspective. In T. R. Gurr (Ed.) *Violence in America: Protest rebellion, and reform* (Vol.2, pp. 201–230). Newbury Park, CA: Sage Publications.

Gurr, T. R. (1998). Terrorism in democracies. In W. Reich (Ed.), *Origins of terrorism: Psychologies, ideologies, theologies, states of minds* (pp. 86–102). Washington, DC: Woodrow Wilson Center Press.

Hamel, J. (2006). Domestic violence: A gender-inclusive conception. In J. Hamel & T. L. Nichols (Eds.), *Family interventions in domestic violence: A handbook of gender inclusive theory and treatment* (pp. 3–26). New York: Springer.

Janis, I. L. (1972). *Victims of groupthink.* New York: Houghton Mifflin.

Kamrava, M. (2005). *The modern Middle East: A political history since the First World War.* Berkeley: University of California Press.

The Kellogg School of Management. (n.d.). Growing up digital: Gen Y technology usage trends. In *The risk of misreading Generation Y: The need for new marketing strategies.* Retrieved September 26, 2008, from http://www.kellogg.northwestern.edu/research/risk/geny/moreabout.htm

Kornadt, H. J. (2002). Biology culture and child rearing: The development of social motives. In H. Keller, Y. H. Poortinga, & A. Scholmerich (Eds.), *Between culture and biology: Perspectives in ontogenetic development* (pp. 191–214). New York: Cambridge University Press.

Lancaster, L. C., & Stillman, D. (2005). *When generations collide: Who they are. Why they clash. How to solve generational puzzle at work.* New York: Collins Business.

Laqueur, W. (1999). *The new terrorism: Fanaticism, and the arms of mass destruction.* New York: Oxford University Press.

Leburn, M. (2009). *Books, blackboards, and bullets: School shootings and violence in America*. Lanham, MD: Rowman & Littlefield Education.

Levin, J. & Fox, J. A. (1999). Making sense of mass murder. In V. B. Van Haslett & M. Hersen (Eds.), *Handbook of psychological approaches with violent offenders: Contemporary strategies and issues* (pp. 173–188). New York: Kluwer Academic.

Madigan, N. (2003, August 31). Cries of activism and terrorism in S.U.V. torching. *New York Times,* p. A2.

Martin, G. (2007). *Essentials of terrorism: Concepts and controversies.* Thousand Oaks, CA: Sage.

Martin, R. J. (2007). Stalking: Prevention and intervention. In E. K. Carll (Ed.), *Trauma psychology: Issues in violence disaster, health, and illness* (pp. 125–146). Westport, CT: Praeger Publishing.

McCauley, C. (2007). Psychological issues in understanding terrorism and the response to terrorism. In B. M. Bongar, L. M. Brown, L. E. Beutler, & P. G. Zimbardo (Eds.), *Psychology of terrorism* (pp. 13–31). New York: Oxford University Press.

McKinley, J. C. & Dao, J. (2009, November 9). Fort Hood gunman gave signals before his rampage. *New York Times,* p. A1.

Meloy, R. (2000). *Violence risk and threat assessment: A practical guide for mental health and criminal justice professionals.* San Diego, CA: Specialized Training Services.

Michael, L. & Herbeck, D. (2001). *American terrorist: Timothy McVeigh & the tragedy at Oklahoma City.* New York: Avon Books.

Moffatt, G. K. (2000). *Blind-sided: Homicide where it is least expected.* Westport, CT: Praeger Publishing.

Newman, K. S. (2004). *Rampage: The social roots of school shootings.* New York: Basic Books.

Nicoletti, J., Spencer-Thomas, S., & Bollinger, C. (2010). *Violence goes to college: The authoritative guide to prevention and intervention* (2nd ed.). Springfield, IL: Charles C. Thomas Publishers.

Oregon State Legislature. (2009). *Oregon State Statute 426.005: Relating to persons who are mentally ill.* Salem, OR: Author.

Post, J. M. (1998). Terrorist psycho-logic: Terrorist behavior as a product of psychological forces. In W. Reich (Ed.), *Origins of terrorism: Psychologies, ideologies, theologies, and states of mind* (pp. 25–40). Washington, DC: Woodrow Wilson Center Press.

Post, J. M. (2007). *The mind of the terrorist: The psychology of terrorism from the IRA to Al-Qaeda.* New York: Palgrave MacMillan.

Purpura, P. P. (2007). *Terrorism and homeland security: An introduction with applications.* Burlington, MA: Butterworth-Heinemann.

Reich, W. (1998). *Origins of terrorism: Psychologies, ideologies, theologies, states of mind.* Washington, DC: Woodrow Wilson Center Press.

Rice, M. E., & Harris, G. T. (1995). Violent recidivism: Assessing predictive validity. *Journal of Consulting and Clinical Psychology, 63*(5), 737–748.

Schrich, L. (2005). *Ritual and symbol in peacebuilding.* Bloomfield, CT: Kumarian Press.

Seligman, K. (2001, June 4). Lone wolf activism: Those who once haunted hate groups blend dangerously into society. *San Francisco Chronicle,* p. A3.

Sheridan, L., & Boon, J. (2002). Stalker typologies: Implications for law enforcement. In J. Boon & L. Sheridan (Eds.), *Psychosexual obsession: Prevention, policing, and treatment* (pp. 63–82). West Sussex, UK: John Wiley & Sons.

Smith, B. L. (1994). *Terrorism in America: Pipe bombs, ad pipe dreams.* Albany, NY: State University of New York Press.

Tarasoff v. Regents of the University of California, 17 Cal. 3d, 425 (1976).

Thomas, D. J. (2011). *Professionalism in policing: An introduction.* Clifton Park, NY: Delmar, Cengage Publishing.

Truman, J. S. (2010). *Communicating terror: The rhetorical dimensions of terror.* Thousand Oaks, CA: Sage Publications.

Vossekuil, B., Fein, R. A., Reddy, M., Borum, R., & Modzeleski, W. (2002). *The final report and findings of the safe school initiative: Implications for the prevention of school attacks in the United States.* Washington, DC: U.S. Secret Service and U.S. Department of Education.

Watkins, M. W., Glutting, J. J., & Youngstrom, E. A. (2005). Issues in subset profile analysis. In D. P. Flanagan & P. L. Harrison (Eds.), *Contemporary intellectual assessment: Theories, tests, and issues* (2nd ed., pp. 251–268). New York: Guilford Press.

White, J. R. (2006). *Terrorism and homeland security* (5th ed.). Belmont, CA: Thomson Higher Education.

Zinn, H. (2003). *Artists in the time of war.* Toronto, Ontario: Hushion House.

Zona, M. A., Palarea, R. E., & Lane, J. C. (1998). Psychiatric diagnosis and the offender-victim typology of stalking. In J. R. Meloy (Ed.), *The psychology of stalking: Clinical and forensic perspective* (pp. 70–87). San Diego, CA: Academic Press.

Zona, M. A., Sharma, K. K., & Lane, J. (1993). A comparative study of erotomanic and obsessional subjects in a forensic sample. *Journal of Forensic Sciences, 38,* 894–903.

The Psychology of Profiling

INTRODUCTION

Criminal profiling is a topic that has taken America by storm and has been glamorized by such shows as *The Profiler* and *Criminal Minds*. These shows allow the novice to obtain a glimpse into the criminal mind and participate in the excitement of the hunt. Finally, what the viewer gets is the satisfaction of catching the killer through a series of clues that can only be detected by the profiler. What television doesn't provide are the skill sets necessary to become an effective profiler. As an investigator, a profiler is looking for a needle in a haystack, and the profiler does not possess extra sensory perception as presented in some television shows or the movies. The skill sets to become an effective profiler are those of a criminal investigator, a psychologist, a crime scene technologist, and a scientist. This chapter will attempt to demystify profiling and conclude by giving you an opportunity to apply your skills by analyzing three letters that I developed and use as training aids in my graduate courses.

WHAT IS CRIMINAL PROFILING?

Criminal profiling goes by many monikers: investigative psychology, criminal profiling, psychological profiling, and offender profiling, yet each is different in its own respect. However, the one thing that stands out is that each attempts to identify a suspect of a crime, or series of crimes, by examining his/her behavior at a crime particular crime scene(s). Profiling has several goals: (1) assist in identifying the suspect, (2) identify personality traits and modus operandi that will make the suspect(s) unique in his particular crime classification, (3) link a series of crimes together by identifying the signature of the offender, and (4) to a much lesser degree, predict future crimes as a form of prevention. Profiling as we know it today is most closely associated with the FBI's Behavioral Sciences Unit (BSU) and its hunt for serial murderers and serial rapists.

UNDERSTANDING THE CRIMINAL MIND

Experts have been attempting to unlock the code to the criminal mind for years. The hunt for the code lies in understanding why someone becomes a criminal, or identifying the causes of criminal behavior. If there is ever such a discovery, then we will have the ability to write a prescription, develop a therapy modality, or change the DNA coding to render the criminal mind helpless. In essence, we would have the ability to create the perfect citizen in much the same way that scientists examine human DNA in an attempt to unlock the code to life and disease. What has prevented this type of success when dealing with the criminal mind is that we are dealing with human behavior, and the variables are vast. It is believed that our personalities are shaped by a triad of environment, psychology, and biology, which can be summed up in one term, *biopsychosocial.*

So when examining the criminal mind, which do you believe to be the most important, understanding the offender's cognitive processes or understanding their behavior? Or would we be better off attempting to understand which had the greater influence on his/her behavior: biology, psychology, or environment? Yochelson and Samenow (1976) assert that the cognitive process is the key to understanding the offender not the offender's behavior. Yochelson and Samenow (1976) discovered that criminals possessed a series of universal personality traits or thinking errors. These errors encompass such things as: fear, lack of self-esteem, pride, the need to feel important, lying, lack of trust, poor decision making, and lack of responsibility/failure to own up to criminal acts (pp. 252–302).

In addition to the aforementioned personality traits, there are three more traits/characteristics that Yochelson and Samenow have identified that remain the cornerstone of most literature today and will to be discussed at length: anger, lack of empathy, and a shut-off mechanism. It should also be noted that these traits have been associated with the psychopathic personality as noted by the research of Dr. Hervey Cleckley in 1941 and Dr. Robert

Hare in 1991 who developed the *Hare Psychopathy Checklist-Revised* which is a psycho-diagnostic instrument used to assess psychopathy.

Anger

Anger is an interesting human emotion. It can be a great motivator in regard to an individual's success or failure. Anger may be directly responsible in the commission of a crime when associated with other emotions such as jealousy or hate; or it may be central when a victim decides that he/she cannot take it anymore and decides to strike back for self-preservation. There are many descriptors for anger; often they are an attempt to quantify an individual's state of mind at the time of an incident. The descriptors used to quantify anger or attempt to describe a subject's state of mind during the commission of a crime are fit of rage, heinous, hate, agitated state, annoyed, furious, disgust, or contempt. Finally, the law classifies violent crime by the act and punishes based on the severity of the act as in the case of murder, rape, armed robbery, or aggravated assault/battery.

Yochelson and Samenow (1976) state that the anger in a criminal metastasizes and is a response to fear, putdowns, an opposing party, and a way to achieve control (pp. 268–270). Keppel and Birnes (1998) classify anger associated with serial killers as clinical anger, which is something that is totally abnormal and is constant rather than transient or situational. The subject never really understands the source of the anger, which increases progressively and exponentially as the subject matures through adolescence to adulthood; there is no compensation for the anger except through a deviant act (pp. 317–318). Beck (1999) asserts that aggressive, manipulative people generally believe that their entitlements and rights override those of others. Hostility, be it from a group or an individual stems from the principle of seeing the adversary as wrong or bad and perceiving self as right. The aggressor construes the facts in his/her favor, exaggerating the transgression, whether imagined or real, and retaliates violently (pp. 125–128). In either definition, anger allows one to justify what she has done by rationalizing the act.

Comments from a Domestic Violence Suspect: "It was her fault. I didn't want to hit her, but she knew how to make me mad. She knows that her job is to have dinner ready for me when I get home from work. I came home today and my damn dinner wasn't ready, so I beat her ass. It's her fault; just ask her."

Comments from a Child Sex Offender: "My girlfriend and I were having problems. I wanted someone to love me, so I had sex with her three-year-old daughter because she loves me no matter what. It wasn't my fault; it was my girlfriend's fault. If she would not have treated me like shit, this would have never happened."

Comments from a Murderer: "He made me mad by disrespecting me in front of my boys. I would have lost my credibility, and everyone would be laughing at me. So I walked up to him in the mall and put two bullets in his head. It was his fault. If he would have never disrespected me, then he would be alive today."

If you analyze the aforementioned statements, what stands out in each case is that the subjects were angry. In each case, the offender had irrational beliefs or standards and was able to rationalize his act. In each of the aforementioned cases, it is about power and control. More importantly, in Beck's description of anger, he notes that the suspect feels entitled and the suspect's rights override the rights of others.

- In the domestic violence case, it was about power and disrespect. The offender is the bread winner, and because of his status, there is an expectation that dinner will be ready. Since dinner was not ready, then it is a sign of disrespect. The suspect rationalizes the violence by stating that it was her fault and she knew the consequences ahead of time.
- In the case of the sex offender, he was angry because his girlfriend cut him off sexually and they were having problems. He views sex as the sole source of love and relationships, not the emotion of love. Because he is not having a sexual relationship with his girlfriend, he is angry. So to show his girlfriend who is in control, he has sex with her three-year-old daughter. However, there is a much deeper issue here. His intent was to have sex with the three-year-old from the beginning, and his personality was such that he was incapable of sustaining a long-term adult relationship with the girlfriend. The alleged failure of the relationship became the excuse.
- In the case of the murderer, he was angry because he felt that his street credibility had been ruined and reputation tarnished. As he stated in my interview with him: "If I did nothing, I would be considered a punk, and then everyone would think they could do that to me." He was embarrassed, which is a fear, and it also speaks to a lack of self-esteem. He rejected the idea of a fist fight with the subject or even an apology because neither made a strong enough statement. The goal was to instill fear in his contemporaries. There was an error in his logic because he ended up in prison where he would have to establish his credibility all over again.

Lack of Empathy

Empathy is a human emotion whereby we have the ability to look at a situation from another's perspective. Empathy should not be confused with the term *sympathy*; rather it should be used as a litmus test to say that we understand the decisions of another, how she came to such a conclusion, and how she thought about the consequences or possible outcomes.

In terms of empathy, an offender who is classified as a psychopath, narcissist, or as having antisocial personality disorder is void of empathy; his goal is gratification and preservation at another's expense (Cleckley, 1982; Hare, 1993).

Cleckley's discussion was specific to the psychopath as we know it today; however, Yochelson and Samenow made the same observation regarding all criminals (pp. 272–274). Vito, Maahs, and Holmes (2007) support the findings of Yochelson and Samenow, noting that criminals tend to be self-centered, hostile, and indifferent to others (p. 128). Walters (1990) argues that the criminal's thought process is irrational and that criminals confuse need with want and are of the belief that what they need entitles them to prey on others to support their lifestyles (p. 137). If you analyze the aforementioned discussion, the thinking is flawed or irrational. The offender's needs far outweigh those of their victims ,with one thought in mind, self-preservation. This is similar to Maslow's hierarchy of needs where the basic needs are primitive and Freud's theory regarding the structure of the personality where the id is responsible for self-preservation and based on the pleasure principle. The goal of each of these is about satisfying one's needs at the cost of others; missing from the personality is the check and balance of guilt or concern for fellow human beings.

Comments from an Armed Robber: "I lost my job, so I have to do what I do. If that means knocking someone in the head to live, then I will. You need to know that I will get mine; to hell with everyone else."

Comments from a Burglar: "I had been watching that house for days. I knew that the guy who lived there was a cripple and needed a wheel chair to get around. I waited for his wife to leave, then I broke in the house. I terrorized that old bastard, and I told him: 'If you call the police, I will kill you. Sit in that damn bed and shit yourself.' I terrorized him repeatedly knowing he couldn't do anything; it just made it more fun. I needed the money. I work, but I don't make enough, so I decided that his money would pay my past-due child support, so that's why I broke in."

Comments from a Drug Dealer and Murderer: "I committed my first murder when I was 12 years old. I killed a kid because he ripped me off stealing my drugs and money. I went to juvenile until I was 16 and was then released. We moved to Florida, and I got back in the drug trade. I was big time and had my own crew, and this bitch ripped me off. She took my drugs, sold them, and kept the money. I gave her three days to get my money. When I went to collect, her boyfriend tried to pull a gun on me, and I killed him. She ran out of the house and got away. I have no regrets. In fact, the only thing that I regret is that I didn't kill that bitch when I had the chance. If I had done that, I would not be in here."

If you analyze the aforementioned statements, what stands out in each case is the subjects' lack empathy and concern for their fellow human being.

Shut-Off Mechanism

I know as reader you have to wonder how someone could harm another individual, yet alone terrorize them. What allows one human being to be so cold as to not recognize that their act(s) are hurting or killing someone else? We all have the potential to commit murder, yet it has to be the circumstances that dictate this ability. Police officers understand their duty and would not hesitate to use deadly force to defend themselves or another. Yet in that situation, oftentimes they are conflicted morally because they have been taught not to kill ,yet legally and because of their oath of office, they have to do the unthinkable. A parent would do the same to protect their child. Yet in each of these instances, it is about protection, and there is usually an aftermath where the officer or parent suffers some psychological trauma. So what is the difference between the criminal and the parent or cop?

The offender's ability to commit such acts is because the offender is believed to have what is known as a shut-off mechanism. This mechanism allows the offender to push fears away from conscious consideration, and it is a critical psychological defense (Yochelson & Samenow, 1976; Hickey, 2002). This mechanism has been discussed by the likes of Freud, Egger, and Lifton all describing what appears to be some out of body experience or dissociative state. Covino (2000) argues that a dissociative state protects the psyche from intense overwhelming experiences (p. 6). The suspect has the ability to block the horror out of her mind to achieve their goal.

In addition to the shut-off mechanism, many criminals use alcohol and drugs to give them courage. The use of drugs and alcohol is the final piece of the puzzle when it comes to placing the mind in a state where the conscience is held in check. Substance abuse provides the subject with the final piece of the courage puzzle, which in effect does nothing more than lower the subject's inhibitions. Bennett and Holloway (2005) note that some offenders abuse substances to excuse their offending behavior (p. 88). Bushman and Cooper (1990) note that there are two motives to drinking—anxiety reduction and power concerns—and when these motives interact with alcohol, they facilitate aggression (p. 342). Hickey (2002) notes that a facilitator may be more than drugs or alcohol such as in the case of a rapist or serial killer; it may well be pornography that fuels a fantasy rather than lower inhibitions (p. 110).

In 1996 the National Institute of Justice conducted a survey of 658 newly convicted male offenders sentenced to the Nebraska Department of Corrections examining four measures of offending associated with illegal drug use the crimes were categorized as: any crime, property crime (burglary, personal robbery, business robbery, theft, auto theft, forgery, and fraud), assault, and drug crime (dealing). The analysis of the data revealed the following:

- The use of illegal drugs was related to all four measures
- During the months of drug use, the odds of committing a property crime increased by 54 percent.
- When using illegal drugs the odds of committing an assault increased by more than 100 percent.
- Illegal drug use increased the odds of committing any crime sixfold (Horney, Osgood, & Marshal, 1996, p. 1).

By no means is this examination meant to be comprehensive. There are a number of explanations that have foundations is the fields of criminology, sociology, criminal justice, psychology, psychiatry, and biology. The goal is to give you the reader some insight into how a criminal thinks. Traditionally, we look at the cognitive process of serial killers or serial rapists. However, my experience has been that many criminals share personality traits/ characteristics, and there is one universal constant: their reasoning is irrational and self-serving.

MOTIVATIONS

Motive as it relates to crime is very difficult to prove because it requires one to understand what the criminal was thinking at the time they committed the offense. During a police investigation, officers are responsible for answering six questions: who, what, where, when, how, and why. In solving many cases, officers can determine the who, what, where, when, and how. Yet the why oftentimes eludes the investigator. Douglas and Douglas (2006) state that behavior reflects personality, and if examined closely crime scene behavior is an extension of one's normal behavioral patterns (p. 32).

The search for motive begins with the victim and their relationships with family, friends, acquaintances, coworkers, finances, enemies, habits/hobbies, activities with and without the family, computer, and cell phone records. The victim's relationship to the crime scene: Why was the victim at this location at that particular time? Or did the crime occur at another location? Von Hertig (2004) notes that the victim shapes and molds the criminal and that their relationship is similar to that of predator and prey. He also argues that to be successful in an investigation, we must be acquainted with the prey as well as the predator (p. 27).

When we think of profiling, we instantly think of the suspect and want to understand their personality deficits as well as why he committed the crime. When we assess grotesque acts of violence from a stance of reasonableness, we want to believe the suspect was psychotic or deranged because there can be no other explanation. Yet in many cases, nothing could be further from the truth. Willie (1974) found that murderers repress their feelings of anger, fear, and aggression, and when they can no longer cope or hide the feelings, they explode (p. 28). Willie also found that there was no difference in murderers who were classified as psychotic and those who were not psychotic and notes that both groups are incapable of processing the information cognitively when it comes to responding to different levels and types of threatening situations (p. 29). It may be because of this deficit that they commit murder. It is understood that anger is but one motivation to commit a crime. Before you move on, take a moment and create your own list of motives that you would associate with violent crime.

Douglas, Burgess, Burgess, and Kessler (2006) offer four general categories of homicide: criminal enterprise, personal use homicide, sexual homicide, and group cause homicide. Each of these categories has a number of subcategories (pp. 93–94). The analysis of Douglas et al. (2006) is associated with murder, yet if we examine the following motivations, in many cases they are universal and can be applied to murder, arson, robbery, financial crimes, burglary and/or rape. The motivations for one to commit a crime are anger, fear, jealousy, revenge, self-preservation, protection, ego, shame, disrespect, love, hate, fantasy, power/control, financial, greed, opportunity, and curiosity. It should be noted that these categories are not mutually exclusive and may be interdependent upon one another during a criminal investigation.

You will have an opportunity to examine two case studies; both are murders with completely different motives, and each is unique to the situation and the individual. Using the information that has been provided, attempt to identify the motive in each of the cases. Also determine if there are any personality deficits that the suspects presented during their interviews noting if the act was out of a perceived need or a necessary want. With that reexamine von Hertig's symbiotic relationship of predator/prey and determine if any of these incidents could have been prevented or if they would happen again if the suspect(s) in questions were not brought to justice?

Case Studies

Case Study Number 1

Leo Boatman Murders

On January 4, 2006, Leo Boatman entered the Ocala National Forest in Ocala, Florida, to go camping. While in the forest he asked a couple for directions to the trail. He describes them as indifferent and pointed in the direction. Boatman noted that the female said little to nothing. He later returned, hid in the bushes, and shot and killed the couple with an AK-47 rifle. He tried to hide the bodies by dragging them into a nearby pond but stated touching the bodies was "gross." Fries (2006) quotes Boatman's friend as saying: "I wouldn't kill a bum because they would have nothing to lose...I went out there and came across two preppie kids and killed them" (p. 1A).

Boatman had been imprisoned or in foster care since the age of 12, and he considered the state his father. He noted that while in prison and foster care he had to create his own world. His escape and passion were murder mysteries where he fantasized about the lead characters. He was also partial to movies like *Silence of the Lambs* and admired Dr. Hannibal Lecter for his intellect. Boatman describes his years of incarceration as being in prison but they were in juvenile detention. He stated that the prison officials described him as a sociopath and they feared he would kill once he was released. He manipulated inmates to fight and officers to provide information regarding their military training keeping detailed notes on how to kill.

In regard to the murders, Boatman felt nothing. In fact, he was excited about the fact that he was being charged with the murders and that it was a death penalty case and cared nothing for the victims. Boatman stated: "I wish I could feel something but I don't. I know that I am supposed to the counselors have told me that, but I can't bullshit you I don't. I don't think about them or their families. I say this knowing that it will probably get me into more trouble." He had only been out of prison four months before he committed these murders. Boatman killed the victims out of curiosity. Boatman also made one very interesting comment regarding his personality, which was, "I feel threatened by people all of the time". In his mind, if a person was indifferent or not nice to him, then they were a candidate to be killed (Marion County Sheriff's Office, Leo Boatman Interviews, 2006).

Analysis of Leo Boatman Murders

1. Was Boatman angry? He had an angry childhood. He was born in a psychiatric facility, and his mother drowned in a ditch when he was eight. Boatman was also bitter because he viewed the state of Florida as his dad, and he suffered abuse in foster care and in juvenile detention. His prior arrests were for burglary and arson. He was angry with the officers and therapists at each of his facilities because they labeled him as a sociopath and believed if released he would kill.

2. Was he empathetic? No. He felt no remorse for his victims. His actions were more about his reputation and the criminal act.

3. Did he possess the shut-off mechanism discussed earlier? Yes. Boatman had the capacity to disassociate his act from his state of being or consciousness.

4. Was he a manipulator? Yes. In his interview, he stated that he started a gang while in prison and later a racist gang only to step away and let them create havoc on other inmates. He states that this was fun. Also he asked officers about their military service and training. The officers opened up, and Boatman cataloged the information as a resource to kill.

5. Did he use alcohol or drugs as a facilitator to commit the crimes? No.

6. What was Boatman's relationship to the victims? None; it was a stranger murder. They were chosen at random.

7. Did anything about the murder bother him? Yes. Initially he attempted to hide the bodies in an adjacent pond; however, touching the bodies grossed him out. Although this was his fantasy, he was a killer still learning. In addition, he stated he would have killed again if he had not been caught. It is believed that he would have overcome this in the next murders as he rationalized the act. This is especially true since he stated killing didn't excite him as much as being caught and facing the death penalty.

8. Was he influenced by movies or books? Yes. His hero is Hannibal Lecter from the movie *Silence of the Lambs*. What he liked most about this character was his intellect.

9. Was Boatman driven by need or want? His desire was want. He wanted to live out a fantasy of killing someone, which he believed would make him famous.

10. Can you recognize any personality deficiencies? Yes. From a clinical diagnosis he would be diagnosed with antisocial personality disorder presenting such features as lack of empathy, inflated ego, inability to conform to social norms, conning of others for personal gain, irritability, and aggressiveness (American Psychiatric Association, 2000).

Classification/Typologies of Crime

In the realm of criminal justice and law, crimes have been classified into two major categories: those that are considered persons crimes and property crimes. In those classifications there is a hierarchy from least serious, which are misdemeanor offenses, to the more serious felonies, be it an act of violence or the value of property. In the United States, the Federal Bureau of Investigation (FBI) narrows the field for reporting the violent felonies, which are murder, robbery, forcible rape, and aggravated assault. Diagram 8-1 is an example of the hierarchy of persons crimes from simple assault, which is a misdemeanor, to murder and its attempts, which are felonies.

The second category of crime the FBI maintains data for are property crimes and include burglary, larceny/theft, motor vehicle theft, and arson. Simply stated, persons crimes are acts of violence against particular victim(s), and property crimes are associated with loss of valuable items where there is no violence. Although I was able to prepare a hierarchy of crimes for violent acts against persons, it would be impossible to do so for property crimes because it is impossible to define one property crime as being more egregious than another.

In the field of profiling there have been a number of attempts to develop a profile based on a particular typology. Theorists like labels because they

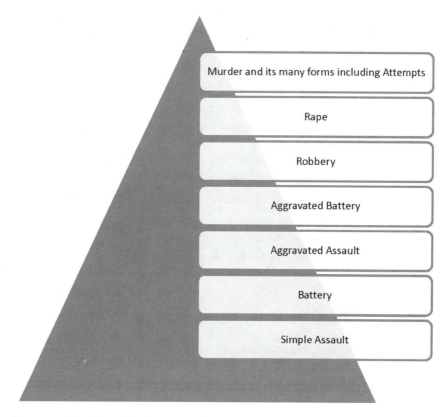

Diagram 8-1: Hierarchy of Persons Crimes

provide them with the ability to explain behavioral patterns. The problem with such typologies is that there will always be a number of subcategories. As Hickey (2002) notes, oftentimes the subcategories overlap or collide with each other (p. 20), not to mention that there is great debate amongst the experts as to which typology is best. From a practical standpoint, it becomes a matter of choice and which works best for the given researcher based on need at the time.

Case Study Number 2

The Winston Gang Murder

On March 10, 2006, at approximately 11:30 P.M. Winston Gang was involved in an argument with his mother's (Jackie) boyfriend Bernard Wells that resulted in the murder of Wells. Winston's mother had been dating Wells for two years and shortly after they met Jackie invited Wells to move into her house, which she shared with her

18-year-old son Winston. Wells was a hustler, a pimp, and abused crack cocaine and alcohol. Wells was known to carry two knifes on his person at all times and had cut the furniture in the past, stabbed Jackie's tire to keep her from leaving the house after an argument, and had pulled a knife on Winston's friend placing the blade against his throat threatening to kill the friend.

Jackie was a nurse and single mother who had been single for a number of years and looked for a mate especially since Winston had graduated from high school and looking to move on. Jackie began using crack cocaine to become a part of Wells lifestyle; she even went as far as to hold drugs for Wells during a traffic stop and was subsequently arrested for possession of crack cocaine. Winston resented the negative impact that Wells had on Jackie, and Wells and Winston had several fights during the two-year period, but each ended without the threat of future violence. In fact, Winston describes the incidents as both walking away after a few blows were exchanged.

Six months prior to the night of March 10, 2006, Winston was attacked after a parade in Tampa. Two unidentified males began to stare at him, which he described as looking through him. In police terms this stare is known as the thousand-yard stare. Winston avoided direct eye contact, fearing it would lead to a fight. They approached Winston and while Winston was fighting one suspect, the second suspect pulled a knife and stabbed Winston between the shoulder blades. The suspect pulled the knife out of Winston's back and before he could stab Winston a second time, a friend intervened and his right arm was slashed from wrist to elbow. Police intervened shortly thereafter with no further injury to either of the parties.

On the night of March 10, Winston came home from work and smelled the odor of crack cocaine coming from Jackie's bedroom. In addition, he heard Jackie and Wells arguing over money. Jackie came out of the room and began talking with Winston. Wells followed shortly, and he and Winston had a brief argument concerning Jackie. Wells left the house then returned and approached Winston. Winston described the stare as a thousand-yard stare the same as the incident in Tampa. Winston also noted that although he and Wells had fought in the past, this different Wells was unwilling to let this go. Winston removed a pocket knife from his right pants pocket partially opening the knife wrapping his fingers around the handle and resting the sharp edge of the knife against the forefinger of his right hand. As Wells approached, he pulled his shirt up as if he were reaching for a knife. Winston grabbed Wells in a bear hug attempting to stop him from pulling what Winston believed to be a knife. Upon grappling with Wells, they fell to the floor. Winston's knife slammed into the knuckle of his right hand nearly severing the finger at the second knuckle with Wells on top of Winston. Winston thought he had been stabbed by Wells and opened his knife and began stabbing Wells in the back. Winston stabbed Wells 14 times. Wells staggered outside and died in the driveway (Thomas, Winston Gang Interview, 2005).

During the interview, the police asked Winston repeatedly how many times he stabbed Wells, and he replied multiple times: "I don't know." Winston attempted to tell the investigators about the incident in Tampa, but they refused to listen.

In his statement, Winston detailed the thousand-yard stare and the fact that he believed Wells was reaching for a knife. During the autopsy, a six-inch knife in a sheath was recovered from Wells right pants pocket. With all of the evidence, Winston was charged with second degree murder. After a detailed analysis of the crime scene and evidence, the state attorney dropped the charges and ruled the case self-defense.

Analysis of Winston Gang Murder

1. Was Winston angry? Winston despised Wells because Wells got Jackie hooked on crack and because she had been arrested holding drugs for Wells. The life that Winston knew with his mother had changed drastically over the past two years. Yet anger was not central to the homicide. The investigators interpreted the number of stab wounds as anger and rage, and they badgered Winston because he could not recall how many times he stabbed Wells. What they failed to ask during the questioning was, Why did you stop stabbing Wells? When I interviewed Winston, he stated: "Wells said: You stabbed me." In addition, Winston stated that Wells stopped struggling, which indicated that Wells was no longer a threat.

2. Was Winston empathetic? Winston apologized on several occasions stating that he did not mean for Wells to die but in the same breath noted that he was afraid because of Well's history and the violent acts he observed Wells perpetrate.

3. Did Winston possess the shut-off mechanism discussed earlier? Yes, but it is much different. Winston possessed the ability to rationalize the incident as if he had done nothing he would be dead.

4. Did Winston have a motive murder? No, although the investigators believed that Winston used the incident to kill Wells and cover up the real motive, anger. In fact he drew his knife just in case but only had it partially open. When they fell to the floor and Winston was cut by his knife. Yet he thought he had been stabbed and in self-defense he stabbed Wells.

5. Was Winston's thinking logical seeing that he was cut with his own knife? No, but based on the following facts, it was realistic: (a) Wells was unable to let the argument go returning to the house. (b) Wells approached Winston and got within three feet of him. (c) Wells pulled his shirt up reaching for what Winston believed to be a knife. (d) Wells was known to carry two knifes on his person and had arrests for carrying concealed weapons. (e) Wells gave Winston the *thousand-yard stare,* something that he experienced six months earlier when he was attacked in Tampa.

6. Was Winston a manipulator? No. However, Wells was.

7. Did the use of alcohol or drugs facilitate the murder? No. Winston tested negative for drugs/ alcohol. However, the medical examiner found cocaine and painkillers in Wells system at levels that are consistent with intoxication/impairment and that probably impaired his judgment in such a way that he was unable to let this argument go.

8. Was Winston influenced by books or movies or did he entertain fantasies? No.
9. Was Winston driven by need or want? He was driven by both the basic need to survive and wanting to stay alive.

Motivations for Case Study Number 1: Leo Boatman

In the case of Leo Boatman, the motivation for his murders were driven by anger, ego, and fantasy. Boatman was angry because of the way he was treated as a child. He notes this when he states: "The state is my father and is responsible for who I am." The second motive is associated with his ego and the need to feel important again noting the significance of being charged in a death penalty case and the status associated with such a case. He also wanted to be off of suicide watch so that he could receive what he believed would be the admiration and respect of his fellow inmates because of the murders. Finally these murders were fantasy driven noting that he would escape the cruel world of foster care and incarceration by reading and daydreaming about the characters in the books. In addition his hero was Hannibal Lecter whom he admired for his intelligence.

Motivations for Case Study Number 2: Winston Gang

In the case of Winston Gang the motivations could be many. However, in an examination of the case, the detectives thought that Gang murdered Wells because Gang was angry because of the way Wells had damaged Gang's family especially his mother based on the number of stab wounds and the history, which would have made have made this domestic. However, when examined closely, Gang was motivated by fear and self-preservation. Although it could be categorized as a domestic, the outstanding the underlying motivations for the murder were fear and self-preservation, which were central to Gang's defense and resulted in the dismissal of the charges. This was made clear when Gang stated in his interview that he stopped stabbing Wells because Wells stopped fighting and stated: "You stabbed me."

CRIME SCENE BEHAVIOR

In an attempt to understand criminal behavior investigators look for behavioral cues when profiling. The Behavioral Sciences Unit of the FBI coined the terms *organized* and *disorganized* crime scene behavior. Douglas et al. (2006) notes that the level of organization or disorganization at a crime scene denotes the sophistication of the offender (p. 10). Cornell, Warren, Hawk, Stafford, Oram, and Pine (1996) compared acts of violence of offenders who were considered psychopaths versus those who were not classifying the acts of violence as instrumental and reactive. In their study, they found that the psychopath had the ability to commit acts of violence in either category instrumental, which is planned and purposeful and associated with organized, yet they were very capable of committing acts of violence that can be classified as reactive and disorganized. However, the group of nonpsychopaths' acts of violence were classified as reactive, the violence was perpetrated against familiar victims, and they perceived the victim as provoking the acts of violence (p. 788). Cornell et al. were careful to note that no one act can determine this classification and that nonpsychopaths are very capable of committing acts of violence that are organized and planned.

Meloy (2000) describes acts of violence as either affective or predatory, which are similar to the terms *organized* versus *disorganized* and *instrumental* or *reactive*. Meloy attaches a number of characteristics to each offender, which distinguishes their behavior and would be evident at a crime scene, or information obtained from interviewing a victim/witnesses, or interviewing the offender. Affective violence is intense, reactive, specific to a threat, short in duration because of the autonomic nervous system limitations, and the goal is to reduce the threat. Whereas predatory violence is planned and purposeful, unlimited in duration because of the lack of autonomic nervous system interaction, there is no threat present, goals are unique to that individual, and there is a lack of emotion (p. 88). Compare the crime scene behaviors of Boatman and Gang and each is markedly different:

- Boatman was a predator who hunted his prey, shot the victims for no reason other than curiosity, and was disappointed because he did not get the rush he had fantasized about for years. The problem with Boatman was that he was *grossed out* when he touched the dead bodies, and his crime scene was very disorganized in that he did not plan the attack, escape, and left untold articles of evidence and was caught due to his lack of preparedness. His goals were unique to only him, which were curiosity and to feed his ego. In the final analysis was Boatman really unprepared or did the murders ultimately give him what he wanted public recognition and status?
- Gang's violence was affective and it was due to a perceived threat. Gang's goal was survival nothing more and nothing less. His belief was that if he did not act, he would die based on the actions of Wells and his history. Gang's response was void of logic because he thought Wells had stabbed him when in fact Gang was responsible for his injury. The crime scene here was very interesting because it offered very little in the way of an active fight there were no tables turned over or furniture damaged. The only evidence of a crime was blood on the carpet where the stabbing occurred, the driveway where Wells collapsed, and the injury to Gang's finger. After the incident Gang threw his knife across the street out of fear. Gang described the incident as lasting less than thirty seconds.

When examining a crime scene it is important to look at all of the evidence and attempt to determine why a suspect did certain things. In the case of a rape and murder did the suspect take the time to clean the scene and the body in an attempt to destroy the evidence? Was the victim bound, gagged, and/or tortured? Are the wounds or injuries antemortem, perimortem, or postmortem? Antemortem wounds/injuries show signs of healing, which indicate that they were inflicted before death. If the antemortem wounds/injuries were inflicted by the suspect, it indicates that the victim was held captive by the suspect for some time. The rate and nature of healing will indicate when the injuries occurred. Perimortem are injuries/wounds that were inflicted at or just before death because there is no evidence of healing. In the case of perimortem wounds /injuries, there will be blood in the fatty tissue around the wound, which indicates the victim was alive at the time they were inflicted. Postmortem wounds display no blood in the fatty tissue and occurred after death.

Weapon Choice

Another aspect of the crime scene behavior is the offenders' choice of weapon. A firearm is rather impersonal and allows a suspect to commit the act of violence from a distance. Again, examine the Leo Boatman murders; they were impersonal and committed at a distance. The only time wounds inflicted would be considered personal is if they are contact wounds, which provide the suspect with a certain degree of personal satisfaction, especially if the victim is bound/gagged. In such a scenario, the suspect has total control and has the power of life or death over the victim. The suspect enjoys watching the victim squirm when the threat of death is imminent. In this case, the suspect pulls the trigger and the hammer of the firearm falls on an empty chamber as if playing Russian roulette with the victim's life. From a victim's perspective it is the anguish and fear that they are going to die at that moment. For the suspect, it is watching the victim's reaction that is exciting and fulfills the suspect's psychological needs.

Other weapons that are more personal are edged weapons or some form of ligature. Both types of instruments provide the suspect with more personal forms of death meaning the suspect must touch the victim to complete the act. Grossman (1995) argues that the ability to kill is based on proxemics, the distance between the victim and perpetrator. Grossman states: "There is a direct relationship between the empathetic and physical proximity of the victim and the resultant difficulty and trauma associated with the kill" (p. 97). In his study of killing distances, Grossman developed a graph noting that the more personal the kill the greater the empathy one has for the victim except in those rare cases where the subject is void of empathy or in a life or death situation such as in war (p. 98).

At the far end of the spectrum is dropping bombs or the firing of artillery shells; here there is no contact with the victim, and in fact, those who carry out such missions look at them as being targets not people/human beings on the receiving end of the bombs. In the middle of the graph are hand grenades or the use of firearms. Although there is distance between the perpetrator and the victim, the perpetrator can see their victim yet finds away to justify the act be it demeaning the victim or the act was necessary to save a life or lives.

Finally, most human beings are reluctant or resistant to kill when a victim is at knife range, requires the use of a ligature, or hand-to-hand combat. In either of these cases it could be associated with war where covert operations are essential to the completion of a mission. Or a solider is out of ammunition and has no other alternative but to use a knife or empty hands to exact death in order to survive. However, in the mind of a criminal, these types of attacks are very personal and allow the perpetrator to exact some form of personal gratification, which may correlate to motive. Finally, in at the very top of Grossman's killing graph are homicides associated with sexual acts. From the perspective of a healthy psyche, sexual murder is inconceivable. Yet from a rapist's or murderer's perspective, the act is about meeting their personal needs, which means the victim is dehumanized, dominated, and the vessel chosen to fulfill a void in the offender's psyche. When thinking of sexual homicide, the instruments of the homicides are usually hands, ligatures, or edged weapons. The ability to commit such acts means the offender possesses the shut-off mechanism or the offender's need outweighs empathy for fellow man. This was highlighted in the Boatman case when he stated: "I have no feelings for the victim."

Victim/Witness Statements

An excellent way of obtaining information regarding the offender's crime scene behavior is to ask questions of the victim and any witnesses if there are any. When dealing with victims and witnesses interviewers must be careful not to make suggestions when conducting interviews with victims and witnesses regarding the identity of the offender. In addition, an interviewer must handle surviving victims with care and understand that asking the victims to recount the incident is asking them to relive every aspect of the horror they endured. Ultimately, the interview may result in retraumatizing the victim. However, if an interviewer can get the victim/witnesses to concentrate on the facts and details of the incident, it will help investigators obtain a clear picture of the offender's crime scene behavior and the offender's modus operandi. Victims can offer detail that goes further than clothing /physical description such as: key phrases or statements; language traits or accents the suspect may have; weapon description; the hand the weapon was held in and mannerisms; what was needed to accomplish the act; demands made of the victim, such as particular statements the suspect demanded the victim to repeat, demanding the victim wear clothing or wigs or carry out a rehearsed set of rituals to successfully commit an act(s).

- In the case of one Michigan rapist who was unable to perform sexually unless the victim's child watched. His victims were single mothers who had young children between ages of five and seven. He would choose his victims ahead of time through surveillance and approach them when they were home alone with their child. He would engage the victims with casual conversation earn their trust while outside of the house and ask if he could use the bathroom. Once in the house he would attack the victim by holding a knife to her throat and order the victim into a bedroom. Once in the bedroom and disrobed the suspect would order the victim to call her child into the bedroom to watch and in each of the three cases he stated: "Bitch if you don't call that bastard in here I will kill you both. First I will start with your baby and make you watch then you will be next". Once the child was in the room the suspect would become erect and rape the victim's multiple times vaginally and anally while the child watched.

Signatures and Modus Operandi

A criminal's signature is usually reserved for violent crimes. Keppel and Birnes (2009) attributes the signature to violent serial offenders noting that for these offenders it's not enough to commit the act of violence but they must personalize it making it unique to that particular offender (p. 10). The signature is something that will never change in fact it will be the same at every crime scene.

- A serial rapist may have as his target white females who are 5'11" with brunette shoulder length hair, brown eyes, small breasts, and average hips. The suspect abducts, rapes, and tortures his victims by inserting a hot curling iron into their vaginal cavity. Yet on this day a black female, 5'5", with short black hair, brown eyes, large breasts and hips is abducted, raped, and tortured vaginally with a hot curling iron. Did the same person commit both rapes?

Although the suspect's preference maybe white females, for some unknown reason, he chose a black female on this night. However, he wants you to know that it is him because his signature is the hot curling iron. Victim selection, location, modus operandi, time of day are variables that will change, but the signature will always be the same in each case (Douglas et al. 2006; Holmes and Holmes, 2009; Keppel and Birnes, 2009). Signatures can occur either postmortem or while the victim is alive depending upon the offender's paraphilia.

What may change over time will be the subject's modus operandi, or method of operation (MO). If we use a serial rapist, he may begin by picking up prostitutes but change the location of his victim selection to the local college campus, a supermarket parking lot, or even begin by burglarizing residences in the middle of the night. The change may be due to police response or the desire for a target rich environment such as a college campus. The key in examining such cases is to look for the signature in an ability to link the cases.

Case Linkage

The concept of linking cases is one that seems relatively easy if they occur in one jurisdiction. However, American policing has the unique distinction of limits due to geographical boundaries meaning that investigating officers rarely share information if they are from different jurisdictions. So if there is a serial rapist working within the confines of a city and moves to the jurisdiction of the sheriff's department or another city then these officers maybe working the same suspect, same case, and never know it. Egger (2002) describes this as linkage blindness (p. 241). The problem of jurisdiction and linkage blindness was discussed by August Vollmer, the father of modern American policing, in 1936 where he describes the need for all police to become state police because criminals had become mobile and were becoming organized. The establishment of one unified force would eliminate the chains of jurisdictional boundaries. Vollmer also advocated a national police force to deal with interstate criminal activity (1936, p. 8).

Just as Vollmer was a visionary in 1936, Detective Pierce Brooks of the Los Angeles Police Department saw the need for law enforcement to have a central data base where violent crimes could be cataloged and compared. Detective Brooks designed the first form of what we now know as Violent Criminal Apprehension Program (ViCAP) (Witzig, 2003). ViCAP was instituted by the FBI in 1985 with the goal of cataloguing and identifying cases with similar cases modus operandi or signatures so that law enforcement agencies can coordinate their investigations and share the information. The limitation of such a system is agency participation, which is strictly voluntary, and if investigators don't see any value in such a system or fear that they will lose the case to another agency or the FBI, they might be reluctant to participate. However, the benefits of such a data base far outweigh the negatives when you consider an agency's ability to be able to close a case. Here are two examples:

- In 1981 a prostitute was beaten and murdered in Grand Rapids, Michigan. She was disrobed and her nude body was thrown into the Grand River. There was no crime scene so it was believed that she was murdered in a van. However, there was a unique signature the offender stabbed the victim twenty-five times, cut the tip of her right nipple off, and skinned her pubic area to the vagina postmortem. The skin and pubic hair remained attached but was a flap of skin. Twenty years later a suspect was apprehended in Chicago with the same signature. The linkage occurred because the Grand Rapids Police Department had enough foresight to submit the information to the FBI database.
- In 2000 a single male was beaten to death in his home in Gainesville, Florida. The victim was gay and was picked up at a local bar by an unknown subject. The suspect and victim bought liquor at the local liquor store and returned to the victim's home and had consensual sex. Sometime during the night or early morning the suspect took a shower and after showering he removed the toilet tank lid and beat the victim to death. The suspect stole the victim's car, cash and credit cards. Two days later the suspect picked up a second victim at a gay bar in Daytona Beach, Florida. This time the attack took place in a local motel with the same signature using the toilet tank lid as a weapon to beat the victim. This victim survived because he was discovered by the cleaning lady. The Gainesville Police Department submitted the case to ViCAP and a similar case was discovered in Ocala, Florida thirty minutes south of Gainesville ten years prior. In interviews the suspect did not admit to the crime in Ocala nor was he charged.

In either case without the use of a central database such as ViCAP the Chicago Police Department would have never been aware of the case in Grand Rapids nor would the Gainesville Police Department have been aware of the case in Ocala, Florida. What is interesting to note in both cases is the length of time between reported homicides to ViCAP. Which begs the question, did these killers stop during that time period or did the agencies suffer from linkage blindness in their thinking? We do know that in both cases the suspects were not imprisoned.

Offender Communication

In the realm of crime, criminals rarely communicate with the police or the press. In most investigations, the crime is committed and the suspect leaves the crime scene while the police investigate looking for an unknown subject. The offenders that communicate with the media or police usually fall into one of these categories:

- Terrorists who send some form of communication after the fact to take responsibility for the crime. In acts of terror, the group is looking to send a message, be it retaliation or to strike fear into the masses by exposing their vulnerability.
- A kidnapper who has chosen his victim for a variety of reasons some of which are money, sexual exploitation, retaliation, and politics. Communication is often accomplished through some form of written communication or a series of telephone calls.
- In the case of a serial rapist or serial killer, these offenders look to challenge the police, get media attention, instill fear in the public, torture the victims' families, and possibly offer some insight into their motivation.

These categories are not mutually exclusive, and they may well intersect meaning you will find a kidnapper who will rape his victims and torture the families with phone calls or letters. One of the most successful at this type of campaign was Dennis Rader who is known as the BTK Killer. The BTK acronym stands for bind, kill, and torture. Gibson (2005) catalogs nineteen different forms of communication that the BTK killer had with media and police, which spanned four decades from 1974 to 2005 including letters, postcards, packages with items taken from the victims, and phone calls (p. 58). Other famous killers who have communicated with police and the media are: the Son of Sam, the DC snipers, the Unabomber, the Zodiac killer, and Jack the Ripper.

Gibson (2004) argues that despite the uniqueness serial murder cases that there are certain content themes and the communication is a symbolic extension of the murders. Themes that Gibson noted were taunts, terrorizing the victims loved ones, threats of future crimes, clues to the killer's identity, issuance of demands, and explanations in regards to motivations (pp. 210–211). However, if we examine Gibson's logic, it's not limited to serial killers it can be applied to any criminal who engages in any form of crime with certain motivations such as a serial rapist, a terrorist, or a kidnapper. In essence, the communication is more than an extension of the crime; it is essential and necessary for the act to be complete. From a psychological standpoint, this is the very essence of the perpetrator's ego. If we go back and examine the psyche of Leo Boatman, the murders weren't as important as the aftermath and the recognition he received as the murderer.

CONSTRUCTING A PROFILE

As a reader you have had an opportunity to explore the process of profiling and what it takes to profile a subject. The remaining part of the chapter is for you the reader to take what you have read and apply it to a profiling exercise.

This exercise is unique in that you will have the opportunity to examine two letters that I developed for my criminal behavior classes. This exercise challenges learners to think outside the box in an attempt to ascertain factual information and speculate on the behavior of the offender. The key is to support your beliefs with facts showing how you came to the conclusions. In this case, you are at a disadvantage because there are no crime scene photos, but if you do this correctly, you will have some idea as to where to begin your hunt for the suspect in question as well as personality traits that are exhibited in the letter. Have fun with the exercise and you will find the analysis of the letters in Appendix B. Complete and analysis of each letter before you combine the information this should allow you to get a clearer picture of the suspect. My experience is most learners combine the information from both without looking at the cases individually and in doing so they miss a lot of the detail. You can use the Internet, other books, and other relevant sources as research material to assist you in this challenge. When you have completed the exercise compare your findings to those in Appendix A. In your assessment develop the information for each letter based on the following checklist:

Victimology Checklist

Who is the victim? Discuss or write everything that you know about the victim. This is paramount to understand who the victim is. Remember as much as we think we might know about a person, we never really know them so we have to check all of these sources in order to get a complete picture.

- What are the victims likes and dislikes?
- When was the last time the victim was seen and where? Also, who was the last person the victim had contact with before disappearing? Does the victim have a habit of disappearing and reappearing after being out of contact for hours or days?
- Does the victim have a cell phone and the cell phone number?
- Is the victim active on social networks such as MySpace, Facebook, YouTube, Flickr, or Twitter, and so forth? How often does the victim update these pages or tweet?
- Has the victim been involved in XXX rated Web sites such as Ashley Madison, Fuckbook, and so forth?
- Has the victim been on any blind dates through these Web sites?
- Does the victim have a diary or journal?
- What is the victim's employment history, including current and past employers? What were the victim's relationships at work, and who were the victim's associates? Were there any problem relationships?

- Is the victim a student? What school do the victim attend? What is the victim's course of study? Who are the victim's associates at school? Is the victim a member of any clubs? What do professors/teachers know about the victim?
- Regarding relationships, what is the victim's lifestyle? Is the victim married or divorced? Does the victim see someone outside of the marriage? If single, who is the victim dating? What is the victim's dating style? Is the victim dating or seeing more than one person and why? Have there been problems in any of the relationships? If so, what are they?
- Depending on the nature of the crime, you may have to examine the victim's finances.
- Canvas the neighborhood to determine what the neighbors know about the victim. Have the neighbors have noticed any unusual occurrences at the victim's residence, or has anyone suspicious been hanging around?
- Check with crime analysis in an attempt to determine if there are any similar crimes in the neighborhood or ones that fit the MO but for some reason were interrupted.
- Check to see if patrol has stopped suspicious subjects in the area and identified them through a field interview.

Crime Scene Behaviors Checklist

Here you want to examine the crime scene photos and or video to determine what happened at the scene and examine the suspect's behavior at the crime scene.

- Is there a crime scene, or are there indications that the crime was committed somewhere else and the victim's body dumped at this location?
- If it is a murder, what are the particulars of the murder? Was the victim's body posed, and if so, how?
- Can you determine the suspect's signature? If so, what is it? Remember that the signature is different than the MO.
- If there are wounds, were they inflicted antemortem, perimortem, or postmortem?
- What were the autopsy findings?
- If your victim is still alive, what can the victim tell you about the suspect's behavior at the scene?
- What is the suspect's weapon of choice? How did he use the weapon? Was the victim injured with the weapon?
- If there were threats, what were they? Try to get the victim to recall the statements exactly as they were stated. What were the suspect's demands, if any?
- Did the suspect have a *tool kit*? A tool kit is a bag similar to a doctor's bag where a suspect carries all of the tools they need to facilitate the crime. A tool

kit may contain duct tape, rope, different types of edged weapons or sharp instruments, gags, ligatures, sex toys, condoms, and tools to assist in a burglary if that is a part of the MO.

- Was the victim tortured, and if so, how?
- Was the violence affective and disorganized? Or was the violence predatory and organized?
- Was the victim raped, and if so, how or with what type of instrument?
- Were there any noticeable paraphilias? Paraphilias are acts of sexual deviance and are unique to the individual. Understand that paraphilias are as vast as the human psyche and this is just a small sampling: sadism, sexual satisfaction from inflicting pain on others; pedophilia, sexual acts with children; vampirism, sexual arousal through the extraction of blood; necrophilia, sex with dead bodies; zoophilia, sex with animals; and coprophilia, sexual arousal through feces, be it eating, excreted upon, or excreting on another (Milner and Dopke, 1997).

Offender Characteristics Checklist

After you have detailed all of the aforementioned information it is time to look at the suspect. You will find some of these questions can and will be answered in victimology and crime scene behavior but they need to be addressed here. When dealing with the suspect it is important to note that this information will be sketchiest because of the lack of known information. Here it is important to support your suppositions and inferences with research detailing referencing data that supports the inferences. The goal is create a snapshot of the offender that will help investigators narrow the possibilities.

- What do the crime scene behaviors tell you about the suspect's personality? Did the suspect act impulsively, or was the act planned?
- Did the suspect leave any form of communication? If so, what was the message? Is this message cryptic?
- Can you detail a psychological disorder based on the crime scene behaviors such as narcissism, psychopathy, or antisocial personality disorder? If so, how did you come to that conclusion?
- Can you determine the motive(s) for the crime?
- Are you aware of any solved cases that are similar, and if so, what are the unique quirks of that individual?
- What are the age, race, and sex of the suspect? How did you come to that conclusion? Race and sex can be determined through DNA if you have any.
- What are the possible locations where the suspect and victim could have interacted? Was the meeting one by chance or planned, and how did you come to this conclusion?
- Did the suspect use a medium such as the Internet to meet the victim?

- Is there a victim preference? Remember when discussing this be leery of linkage blindness and look at the signature to rule victims in or out.
- If it is a sex crime, is there a particular paraphilia that the suspect exhibited?
- Whether the suspect right or left handed can be determined in the autopsy or with victim statements.
- What evidence did the suspect leave at the crime scene, and what evidence did the suspect take away from the crime scene?
- Did the suspect take any trophies such as a driver's license, shoes, underwear, a lock of hair, body part, or jewelry?

Below is the first of two letters left by the suspect. The letter is entitled "Letter to Eve." The suspect left the letter after breaking into the victim's home. Also, I have included crime scene information that includes behavior and findings. Read the letter several times and use the checklists, gleaning as much information as you can in reference to the victim and the suspect. Upon completion of the first analysis, a picture should begin to emerge regarding the suspect's personality and his victim choice. Finally, keep in mind that you are at a disadvantage because you do not have access to photos or video.

Letter to Eve

Eve:

How are you? I have been watching you. You have a nice tight body and that dark hair drives me wild.

YOU PROBABLY WANT TO KNOW WHY I CALL YOU EVE IT IS BECAUSE YOU ARE SHORT AND REMIND ME OF THE STORY OF ADAM AND EVE. Eve had to be short to come from ADAMS RIB.

AS I watch you in the shawer, in the bed and I get school it drives me wild. Friday I touched you as you walked by. I thought of you all weekend and I couldn't find you, you were gone missing. So I had to enter your house.

Lay in your bed and smell you.

I WANT HERT YOU. I NEED YOU. PLAESE LOVE ME.

ILL BE WITCHING YOU.

LUV

ME

Crime Scene One "Eve"

Victim(s): Martha Smith   **Sex/Race:** W/F
Address: 1621 North Big Pine Road   **City/State:** Anywhere, USA
Phone: (123) 456-7890

The house is occupied by two white females. However, the suspect only entered the room of Martha Smith. Martha is a student at the local college majoring in legal studies. Items recovered:

1. A hanger from the front door. It appears that the hanger was used to break into the home. There is nothing unusual about the hanger and can be found at any local cleaners.
2. One navy blue Nike T-shirt. The shirt was cut from the bottom center toward the neckline. There were also two slits located at breast level. The shirt was not soiled nor were there any stains on the shirt. The T-shirt belongs to the victim.
3. One pair of Gilligan & O'Malley pink panties size XL that belong to the victim. The panties were located on the bed just below the T-shirt as if they were laid out to be worn later.
4. A letter to Eve. The only fingerprints located were found on the letter. They have been run through AFIS and there is no record on file in any database.

Below is the second of two letters left by the suspect. The letter is entitled "Dear Mel." The suspect left this letter exactly seven days after breaking into the first victim's home. Also I have included crime scene information that includes behavior and findings. The MO of the burglary was exactly the same except this time the suspect left a bloody palm print on the window; however, there was no sign of forced entry. As with the first read the letter several times and use the checklists gleaning as much information as you can in reference to the victim and the suspect. Upon completion of this analysis the picture of the suspect's personality and his victim choice should become clearer. Remember you are at a disadvantage because you do not have access to photos or video.

Dear Mel

Dear Mel:

Your name is not MEL anymore I will refer to you as MARY M. the

first. You know that EVE WAS A BITCH. She would not acknowledge my presence. She is luky that I don't hert her or that boyfriend of hers. iT may still happen if you hert me.

Mary I need you. IF YOU ARE SMART AND I KNOW YOU ARE, YOU NEED TO FIGURE OUT WHY I CALL YOU maRY. I'V SEEN you with YOUR BOYFRIEND, MAKING LOVE IN THAT BED, HOW COULD YOU?!!!!!!! when YOU KNOW THAT I LOVE YOU. How could u take a shower with him, when you know that I luv you. If i see you with him again something bad will happen!!!!. You are mine and u know that. How could you tease me, smile at me, kiss me and make luv to me and then go back and do the same thing with him. You are truly MARY M. I left you these panties they have something in tem, I like to call it my pimp juice. Wear them when you sleep at night then I will be with you at night my pimp juice placed against my woman, and don't forget that.

Loving AND SMELLING your sex,

THE MAC

Crime Scene Two "Dear Jules"

Victim(s): Melanie Thomas   **Sex/Race:** W/F
Address: 1621 North Big Pine Road   **City/State:** Anywhere, USA
Phone: (123)456-7890

The house is occupied by two white females. This is the second incident at this address with the suspect targeting roommate #2, Melanie Thomas. Melanie is a student at the local college majoring in Forensic Science. Items recovered:

1. A hanger from the front door. It appears that the hanger was used to break into the home. There is nothing unusual about the hanger and can be found at any local cleaners. This was the same method of entry as in the first incident.
2. One white T-shirt with a blue ring around the neckline. The shirt was cut from the bottom center toward the neckline. There were also two slits located at breast level. Unlike the first incident, this T-shirt was soiled with B+ blood and it has been determined that it is that of a white male. There were blood stains on either side of the cut in the center of the T-shirt. In addition there were two slits located at breast level of the T-shirt with blood stains at each slit. This blood matched the blood located on the center of the shirt. The T-shirt belongs to the victim.
3. One pair of Haines purple panties size medium, which belong to the victim. The panties were located on the bed just below the T-shirt as if they were laid out to be worn later. However, these panties are soiled with epithelials, semen, blood, and Vaseline. It appears that the suspect masturbated in the panties. The samples all match the unknown white male suspect.
4. A letter to Mel contained five bloody fingerprints. These prints match the prints found at Crime Scene One. There was also a bloody palm print located on the bathroom vanity as well as on the bathroom window. The prints have been run through AFIS and there is no record on file in any database.
5. All of the blood samples of blood semen and hair come from the same individual. The fingerprints from the two scenes are from the same suspect.

CONCLUSION

Profiling has been described as an art by some, and others look at it as wasted effort or voodoo because it is not an exact science such as math or chemistry. I have to admit that when I see a profiler on the national networks after a kidnapping or murder because they have very little to offer. Yet the networks seek these experts out because it makes the bystander watch that particular news channel.

Profiling is a skill set that is learned through hours of study of crime scenes, a working knowledge of psychology, victimology, the ability to discern crime scene behaviors, and the analysis of countless interviews with suspects, victims, and witnesses. The two final ingredients to the process are the ability think abstractly and apply what has been learned to real-world cases.

As a professor, I wanted you to experience the challenges that a profiler is faced with, so I created the analysis of the letters for you the reader. I hope that you enjoyed the task. Please examine the analysis of the letters in Appendix B: Criminal Profile of the Mack to see how well you did and if you measure up to the task.

REFERENCES

American Psychiatric Association. (2000). *Diagnostic and statistical manual of mental disorders: Text revision* (4th ed.) Washington, DC: Author.

Beck, A. T. (1999). *Prisoner's of hate: The cognitive basis of anger, hostility, and violence.* New York: HarperCollins Publishers.

Bennett, T. & Holloway, K. (2005). *Understanding drugs, alcohol, and crime.* New York: Open University Press.

Bushman, B. J. & Cooper, H. M. (1990). Effects of alcohol on human aggression: An integrative research review. *Psychological Bulletin, 107*(3), 341–354.

Cleckley, H. M. (1982). *The mask of sanity.* St. Louis, MO: The C. V. Mosby Company.

Cornell, D. G., Warren, J., Hawk, G., Stafford, E., Oram , G., & Pine, D. (1996). Psychopathy in instrumental and reactive violent offenders. *Journal of Consulting and Clinical Psychology, 64*(4), 783–790.

Covino, N. A. (2000). Dissociation: elements, history, and controversies. In L. Sanchez-Plannell & C. Diaz-Quevedo (Eds.), *Dissociative states,* pp. 1–20. Barcelona, Spain: Springer-Verlag Iberica.

Douglas, J. E., Burgess, A. W., Burgess, A. G., & Kessler., R. K. (2006). *Crime classification manual.* San Francisco, CA: John Wiley and Sons.

Douglas, J. E. & Douglas, L. K. (2006). The detection of staging, undoing, and personation at the crime scene. In J. E. Douglas, A. W. Burgess, A. G. Burgess, & R. K. Kessler (Eds.), *Crime classification manual* (2nd ed., pp. 31–44). San Francisco, CA: John Wiley and Sons.

Egger, S. A. (2002). *The killers among us: An examination of serial murder and its investigation.* Upper Saddle River, NJ: Prentice Hall.

Fries, J. H. (2006, January 12). From troubled boy top camper's killer? *St. Petersburg Times,* p. A 1.

Gibson, D. C. (2004). *Clues from the killers: Serial murders and crime scene messages.* Westport, CT: Praeger Publishing.

Gibson, D. C. (2005). B.T.K. strangler versus Wichita Police Department: The significance of serial murder media relations. *Public Relations Review 32,* 56–65.

Grossman, D. (1995). *On killing: The psychological cost of learning to kill in war and society.* New York: Little, Brown & Co.

Hare, R. D. (1991). *The hare psychopathy checklist-revised manual.* North Tonawanda, NY: Multi-Health Systems.

Hare, R. D. (1993). *Without conscience.* New York: Guilford Publications.

Hickey, E. W. (2002). *Serial murderers and their victims* (3rd ed.). Belmont, CA: Wadsworth/Thomson Learning.

Holmes, R. M. & Holmes, S. T. (2009). *Profiling violent offenders: An investigative tool* (4th ed.). Los Angeles, CA: Sage Publications.

Horney, J., Osgood, D. W., & Marshall, I. H. (1996). *Adult patterns of criminal behavior.* Washington, DC: National Institute of Justice.

Keppel, R. D., & Birnes, W. J. (1998). *Signature killers: Interpreting the calling cards of the serial murderer.* New York: Pocket Books.

Keppel, R. D., & Birnes, W. J. (2009). *Serial violence: Analysis of modus operandi and signature characteristics of serial killers.* Boca Raton, FL: CRC Press.

Marion County Sheriff's Office. (2006). *Leo Boatman interview: Case number 06001267.* Ocala, FL: Author.

Meloy, J. R. (2000). *Violence risk and threat assessment: A practical guide for mental health and criminal justice professionals.* San Diego, CA: Specialized Training Services.

Milner, J. S., & Dopke, C. A. (1997). Paraphilia not otherwise specified: Psychopathology and theory. In D. R. Laws & W. O'Donohue (Eds.), *Sexual deviance: Theory, assessment, and treatment* (pp. 394–423). New York: Guilford Press.

Thomas, D. J. (2005). *Winston Gang Interview: Case number 5050354.* Clearwater, FL. Author.

Vito, G. F., Maahs, J. R., & Holmes, R. M. (2007). *Criminology: Theory, research, and policy* (2nd ed.). Sudbury, MA: Jones and Bartlett Publishers.

Vollmer, A. (1936). *The police and modern society.* Berkeley: Regents of the University of California.

von Hertig, H. (2004). The criminal and his victim. In J. E. Jacoby (Ed.), *Classics of criminology* (3rd ed., pp. 27–29). Long Grove, IL: Waveland Press.

Walters, G. D. (1990). *The criminal lifestyle: Patterns of serious criminal conduct.* Newbury Park, CA: Sage Publications.

Willie, W. (1974). *Citizens who commit murder.* St. Louis, MO: Warren H. Green.

Witzig, E. W. (2003). The new ViCAP more user-friendly and used by more agencies. *FBI Law Enforcement Bulletin, 72*(6), 1–12.

Yochelson, S., & Samenow, S. E. (1976). *The criminal personality—Volume I: A profile for change.* Lanham, MD: Rowman & Littlefield Publishers.

Conclusion

INTRODUCTION

As reader you have had the opportunity to examine the field of police psychology from two perspectives: the officer in need of psychological services and the use of psychological principles as a tool in relationship to the criminal mind. When I think of police psychology, it can best be described as one of the many components that have been instrumental in transitioning policing from a trade to a profession. However, the field of psychology is one that is questioned by professional officers and administrators alike because it is not exact and, in most cases, is administered by outsiders. To emphasize the uncertainty regarding the use of psychology in the hiring process, let's reexamine the quote in chapter 1 from the chief of a midsize police department: "I know people; after I review their hiring packet and personally interview them, I can tell you if they have a psychological problem. All the damn psychologist is going to do is administer a test, score it, and tell me if the person is a suitable candidate, all for $200, and that's money I can use for something else."

A NEW SPECIALTY: DEFINING SERVICES

Although the field of psychology has been around for years, police psychology is a relatively new specialty evolving from preemployment assessments and psychological services in the late 1960s to an ever-increasing role today, which includes career development and the application of psychological principles to such areas as criminal profiling, hostage negotiations, and eye-witness identification (Scrivner & Kurke, 1995).

In reviewing the research, it is clear that agencies are unclear as to what they want when it comes to mental health services. In informal interviews I conducted with chiefs, they mentioned that they have services and that those services are confidential. When I asked them to detail the services, they told me: "If our guys are involved in a shooting, then they see the shrink; if they have family problems, they can see the shrink; if I need to know if they are fit for duty, I send them to the shrink; and the shrink provides us with the recommendations as to who passed or failed their psychological test during the hiring process; that's all we need." When asked whether they use the same mental health professional for all of the services, 10 out of 10 chiefs advised that they do. I then asked whether they see a conflict of interest when officers seek counseling services and then see the same professional when it comes to a fit-for-duty evaluation. In each case, my question was met with silence; they answered yes but indicated that it was something they had never considered. In essence, police administrators must become informed consumers specifying their needs.

THE APPLICATION OF PSYCHOLOGY TO POLICING

When I started my career in 1978, I had just graduated from college with a bachelor's degree in psychology and thought I knew it all. However, my first training officer was a veteran officer and had as many years on the department as I was old, 22. He was a master manipulator with a silver tongue, and there were no boundaries when it came to race or gender; he knew people. He advised me that the streets were my new college. He also stated: "Most of the theories you studied are just that; what you will learn here, kid, is that this job is about meeting people's needs in a time of crisis, and the skill set is gained through practice."

In many ways, he was correct. If we go back and examine chapters 5 and 6, we see that being successful involves more than just education; it involves practice. Being a great interrogator or negotiator it is about training and continual development of the skill set. Chapters 7 and 8 are slightly different, but the skill set is the same; officers become good or exceptional in the area of threat assessment and profiling only through experience and exposure. In any of the aforementioned specialties, it is not enough to be just an officer; success is dependent upon education, training, research, and emersion in the types of cases that allow the officer to develop their skills.

THE FUTURE

The future of police psychology is bright. To sell the process and the science to officers, the practitioners must participate in ride alongs to change the perception of psychology, participate in training, and specify what services they are comfortable with and outline any issues they foresee as a conflict of interest.

Since the days of August Vollmer, the effort to have policing accepted as a profession has been ongoing. What seems to have hampered the effort is a series of poor decisions that can be traced back to the police personality. The example that I refer to is a desire not to follow the established standards set forth by the courts, especially in such areas as Miranda or search and seizure. The concept of catching the bad guy is all well and good, but not to the exclusion of the rules and the profession. The same applies when we speak of acts of brutality or overt racism. We all understand how one can become biased or will do anything to get the bad guy. As you reflect on the discussion of the police personality, answer the following question: If you were an administrator, what steps would you take to keep officers' personal issues from becoming a factor in their professional lives?

From an administrative standpoint, the agency must become more sensitive to officers' mental health needs; inform officers during training sessions about the services that are available, rather than just hand out pamphlets; and review policies and procedures regarding fit-for-duty evaluations. In many instances, when officers speak of mental health needs there is a stigma attached. Remember the three case studies in chapter 3; each officer had a problem with the services and was worried about being labeled as weak. In fact, labeling provides great insight into the persona of the profession.

In addition to traditional police mental health issues, policing is experiencing a new dilemma—the returning war hero. The number of officers who have been called to active duty to fight in Iraq and Afghanistan is unprecedented. In these conflicts, they have been experiencing and have been called on to do things that only those serving in war zones will ever face. With those actions comes an exposure to trauma that far exceeds what many officers will see over the course of a 20-year career. Experience tells us that these returning officers will have some problems adjusting to daily living, so the question becomes: How will this impact them as officers on the road? The greater question here is whether the agencies are prepared to work with these heroes so that they can make a smooth transition from professional soldiering to professional policing.

I opened this section with the statement the future of police psychology is bright. I truly believe that, yet as noted, it is a skill set that needs to come out of the closet within agencies. The ideal program would begin with an agency's mental health professionals meeting with new officers and their families during new officer orientation to address the following: advising the spouses and family members of the stresses of the profession and the impact that the field-training officer program will have on the new officer; providing insight into the police personality and some of the changes that might take place in the new officer; discussing the impact of shift work; and finally, emphasizing that the services are for the family, not just the officer.

However, the involvement of service providers should not stop there. They should also be involved in training; provide consultation in such areas as hostage negotiation, the selection of SWAT team members, and development of a critical incident stress management (CISM); and assist in career development. Finally, there are two areas that are often overlooked: career development and the retirement years. Career development speaks for itself, and the role here is to assist an officer in developing a career path. Policing is a unique animal in that most officers don't have a plan when they retire. Many can retire in their early forties, so what should they do? If an officer is planning to retire, then five years prior to retirement, a mechanism needs to be in place so the officer can plan a future outside of policing. The most difficult of task for this group is giving up that identity and moving on.

CONCLUSION

There is undoubtedly an uneasy alliance between police and psychology. What everyone has to realize is that the sooner police accept that police psychology is here to stay, the sooner this alliance can become healthy and grow. The keys are exposure to mental health professionals, understanding the rules, and making an effort to remove the stigma associated with mental health services. Much of this can take place in a training environment, during ride alongs, and by having mental health professionals acting in the capacity of consultants. Finally, it should be noted that when selecting a mental health professional for an agency, the agency and the union should shop for the best fit. If a mental health professional or group is selected because of low bid or politics, it can be more destructive than offering no services.

REFERENCE

Scrivner, E. M., & Kurke, M. I. (1995). Police psychology at the dawn of the 21st century. In M. I. Kurke & E. M. Scrivner (Eds.), *Police psychology into the 21st century* (pp. 3–30). Hillsdale, NJ: Lawrence Erlbaum Associates.

Appendix A:
Triple Homicide Interview

Scenario 6-1 (extended version)

Investigator   Hello, Tom; how are you? I am Investigator Ferris; have a seat.

Response   Why am I here in Homicide? I was arrested and booked on attempted burglary, possession of burglary tools, and carrying a concealed weapon.

Investigator   Hey, Tom, we just want to talk to you about the burglary. I am going to read you your rights before we do anything.

Response   I already know my rights. I will talk to you, but I ain't got nothing to say. I still don't understand why I am here in Homicide.

Investigator   Like I said, we just want to talk.

Response   OK, what do you want to know?

Investigator   Tom, it was 12:00 in the morning. Why were you breaking in the house so late?

Response   Because at night no one can see you and I am free to roam.

Investigator   But at night you run the risk of being discovered by the home owner.

Response   I am not worried about that because I am quiet like a cat on the prowl.

Investigator   I notice that you said you like to roam at night and you are like a cat—is that important to you?

Response   Yeah, because it means I can do something no one else can. C'mon you know the thrill in something like this is not getting caught.

Investigator	So how did you choose this house out of all the houses in the neighborhood?
Response	I don't know; it was random. I just started roaming, saw the house was dark as well as those around it, and thought it would be a good house to break into.
Investigator	Besides the excitement of the prowl, what were you hoping to take from the house?
Response	I was going to go into each family member's room and stand over them while they slept and then take things like jewelry and money.
Investigator	That's it, just jewelry and money?
Response	Yeah, and that girl they have, I wanted to see her close up.
Investigator	Tom, I am confused. I thought you said you chose the house at random?
Response	Uh, yeah, I did.
Investigator	So how do you know if there is a girl at all?
Response	Er, I am just guessing. It's a family, isn't it?
Investigator	OK, Tom, let's go back. You said you like to stand over families while they sleep?
Response	Sure, I am in their house robbing them blind, and they have no idea that I'm there. What's even more fun is standing over them knowing that I am in control. What a rush.
Investigator	What happens if someone wakes up while you are standing over them?
Response	That's why I have the knife, rope, and tape.
Investigator	Why do you carry those with you?
Response	You know why I carry those; you ain't stupid.
Investigator	No, I don't; that's why I am asking.
Response	I carry them so if someone wakes up, I can threaten him with the knife, tie him up, and tape his mouth shut.
Investigator	Why not run?
Response	If I run, they can call the police. If I tie them up, they have to stay that way until someone finds them.
Investigator	So do you just tie up the one who wakes up or what?
Response	No. If one wakes up, that means even when I tie him up that he can still make noise and wake the others. So everyone in the house has to be tied up.
Investigator	So how would you do this to keep each one from waking?
Response	Man, why would I tell you that?
Investigator	Tom, I have to say that I am learning something here. The only things we have on you are the charges you mentioned when you first sat down. You will get bond and be out of here, and you know that there is no violence here, so you won't get any jail time.

Response	OK, man. I would have a room in the house set up with chairs so that I could secure them one at a time. Starting with the man of the house because he is most dangerous. After everyone is secure, I have all night to take what I want and then leave the house without being caught.
Investigator	Tom, I want to thank you for sharing. I have just a few more questions, and then I will have them take you back to your cell. Tom, how good is your memory?
Response	It's pretty good.
Investigator	Can you remember as far back as six months ago?
Response	Not sure; it depends on what you are talking about.
Investigator	Well, there was a burglary, and the suspect did exactly what you described you would do.
Response	I have no idea what you are talking about.
Investigator	Tom, have you told anyone else about the burglaries and what you do once in the house?
Response	No, its all me; that's my idea.
Investigator	So what I have here is a burglary where someone stole your idea, or it was you.
Response	Can you tell me what happened at that crime scene?
Investigator	Tom, c'mon, you know I can't do that. If you didn't do it, then you didn't do it. What that means is that someone else is taking credit for your work. Do you want that?

The interview stops here because we are at a crossroad. If you pressure Tom here, he may well stop talking and demand an attorney. As an investigator, you don't know if Tom has committed more burglaries than just this one. Prior to this interview, a check with adjoining jurisdictions should have been done to see if there is anything that fits the modus operandi. It could be short of the murder, and if so, may well be practice on the part of the suspect in developing his skill set and confidence. There may also be one or two burglaries that have not been reported to the police. The last question is an open-ended one so that Tom may agree to discuss his previous crimes, which may ultimately lead the investigator back to the triple homicide. The key is never to reveal the hidden crime facts.

Appendix B:
Criminal Profile of the Mack

VICTIMOLOGY: This is the first step of the profile, an examination of the victims. There are two victims linked to the case based on the evidence, and this analysis will show how they are linked and if there is a relationship to the suspect.

Victim One: Martha Smith, W/F, 5'6", 120 lbs., 21 years old, brown hair, blue eyes. Address: 1621 North Big Pine Road; City/State: Anywhere, USA; Phone: (123) 456-7890.

Victim one is a student at the local college majoring in legal studies and rooms with another student, Melanie Thomas. Victim one has a boyfriend, and they usually spend the night together at her house or his four to five nights a week. Victim one is active in school organizations and is a member of a sorority. Her boyfriend was ruled out as a possible suspect because he was with her at the time of the burglary and his fingerprints don't match those left at the scene. Victim one was asked of her past relationships before this boyfriend, and there weren't any. She has been with this boyfriend since they began school three years ago. She was asked if she had cheated on her current boyfriend, and she replied, "No." Victim one has not had any unusual contacts with anyone and stated that when she goes out with her friends, they do everything together. She went so far as to state that she hasn't even danced with another person since she has been in the relationship with her boyfriend.

Friends and members of the university organizations support victim one's assertions and observations. Victim one has stated that she felt as if someone had been watching her but blew it off. She stated that she had the feeling when she was entering her residence and would look around and found nothing.

In regards to the letter to Eve, victim one states that she came home and found a hanger hanging from the door knob of the front door and the door standing wide open. Before entering, she called out to her roommate. There was no response, so she entered the residence and found no one there. However, she did find a pair of her panties and a T-shirt laid out on the bed along with the letter to Eve, and she immediately called the police.

AN ANALYSIS OF THE LETTER REVEALS THE FOLLOWING

The suspect has chosen the victim because she fits what he believes to be his ideal partner: short, dark hair, and a tight body. This is supported in the first sentence where the suspect states: "You have a nice tight body and that dark hair drives me wild."

The suspect appears to have been stalking the victim for some time and knows her schedule, where she frequents, and her associates. This is supported in the first paragraph where the suspect states: "I have been watching you." This is also supported in the third paragraph where the suspect states: "AS I watch you in the shawer, in the bed and I get school it drives me wild. Friday I touched you as you walked by. I thought of you all weekend and I couldn't find you, you were gone missing. So I had to enter your house." He makes note of every place he observes the victim. The suspect mentions that he watches victim one in the shower; this has been ruled out because there are no windows and no cameras were found in a thorough search of the bathroom and bedroom.

At this crime scene, the suspect acknowledges that he laid in victim one's bed and smelled her as if he were attempting to take in her essence. The suspect states that he loves the victim and that he won't hurt her, which is supported in paragraph four where the suspect states: "I WANT HERT YOU. I NEED YOU. PLAESE LOVE ME." The suspect states that he touched victim one as she walked by on Friday. The victim states that she was in school all day Friday and that is the only place the suspect could have touched her. After that, she left and went out of town with her boyfriend for the weekend. This further supports the notion that the suspect has been watching victim one and that he has access to the victim on the campus. Victim one states that there was nothing unusual about someone touching or bumping into her and that she does not recall any such incident.

The suspect has chosen to change victim one's name to Eve. This is interesting because Eve is the first woman in the Bible, and it may have more of a meaning—such as Eve being the temptress in the Garden of Eden, or victim one being the first in a series of victims. It is clear that the suspect is delusional because he states that he loves victim one, yet he has had no personal contact with victim one. A suspect such as this is lacking in social skills because if he were in love with victim one, he would not be a voyeur. The suspect closed the letter with the words: "Luv Me," as if to say you know me. Finally, there are a number of misspelled words in this letter. I refrain from making a judgment at this time; this could be intentional or a ploy to throw off investigators.

CRIME SCENE BEHAVIOR

The suspect gained entry by burglarizing the front door of the residence using a hanger that can be obtained at any cleaners. The door is loose, and the lock is a key-in-the-knob lock, which was easily manipulated. Once in the house, the suspect entered victim one's bedroom, went through her dresser drawers to find the underwear and T-shirt drawers, and removed one pair of panties and one T-shirt. The suspect laid in victim one's bed and fantasized about having sex with her. The suspect then laid the T-shirt and panties out for victim one. The suspect has never been arrested because he was not afraid to leave his fingerprints at the crime scene.

Victim Two: Melanie Thomas, W/F, 5'9", 130 lbs., 24 years old, blonde hair, brown eyes. Address: 1621 North Big Pine Road; City/State: Anywhere, USA; Phone: (123) 456-7890.

Victim two is a student at the local college majoring in forensic science and rooms with victim number one, Martha Smith. Melanie has a boyfriend (John Rouse), and this is her second boyfriend since being enrolled at the university. She has been with boyfriend John for the past two years. Her first boyfriend was Tony Barringer, a popular college football player. Victim two states that she and Tony are still friends and talk occasionally. Victim two also advises that Tony has moved on and is very happy with his current girl-friend. The fingerprints left at the crime scene along with other evidence rule out Tony Barringer and John Rouse as suspects. Victim two has cheated on John with three other individuals since they have been together. Victim two discounts that these three would have anything to do with such an incident. These three suspects were interviewed and ruled out because they had alibis and their fingerprints and the evidence did not match them. Victim two is a member of the same organizations as victim one, and they run in the same circle of friends, which rules out any associates or acquaintances.

This is the second incident at this address. The first occurred approximately seven days prior to this incident. In regard to the letter entitled "Dear Mel," victim two states that she came home and found a hanger hanging from the door knob of the front door and the door standing wide open. This MO is exactly the same as the first burglary. Before entering, she called out to her roommate. There was no response, so she entered the residence and found no one there. However, she did find a pair of her panties and a T-shirt laid out on the bed along with the letter to Mel. There was one distinct difference in the clothing; the T-shirt was cut from the bottom up in the front center. There was a slit on each side at nipple length, and each of the cuts was covered in blood. In addition, the panties were blood stained. Victim two called police immediately.

AN ANALYSIS OF THE LETTER REVEALS THE FOLLOWING

Unlike victim one, the suspect does not describe victim two's body size, body type, hair color, or eyes. He has chosen this victim because victim one refused to acknowledge his presence and in fact has ignored the suspect based on his delusions. This incident serves as a threat and puts both victims on notice. This is supported in the second paragraph in which the suspect states: "You know that EVE WAS A BITCH. She would not acknowledge my presence. She is luky that I don't hert her or that boyfriend of hers. iT may still happen if you hert me."

Because both victims run in the same circles and have the same friends, it appears that the suspect has been able to stalk them both. Also, the suspect references victim two's boyfriend and seeing them together and has observed them having sex in the bed and shower. The suspect continues to exhibit delusional belief systems in that he tells victim two he "luvs" her. This is supported in third paragraph where the suspect states: "I'V SEEN you with YOUR BOYFRIEND, MAKING LOVE IN THAT BED, HOW COULD YOU?!!!!!! when YOU KNOW THAT I LOVE YOU. How could u take a shower with him, when you know that I luv you."

As in the first letter, the suspect alludes to the fact that he observes victim two having sex with her boyfriend. There is a window in victim two's bedroom as well as a window in her bathroom. Yet both are covered with blinds and have frosted glass, which makes them impossible to see through. Victims two's bedroom and bathroom were checked for cameras, and there were none. However, this does not exclude the suspect following victim two home and listening through the bedroom window or shower window. Both victims acknowledge that they have had sex with their respective partners while in the shower and in bed.

This letter is much more aggressive in that the suspect claims ownership, is delusional, and threatens victim two. This is supported in paragraph three where the suspect states: "If i see you with him again something bad will happen!!!!. You are mine and u know that. How could you tease me, smile at me, kiss me and make luv to me and then go back and do the same thing with him." Since victim two's other lovers have been ruled out; the suspect is delusional when he states that victim two has betrayed him noting that victim two teased him, smiled at him, kissed him, and made "luv" to him. Again, victim two has no idea who this suspect is, and it is believed based on the first letter that the suspect has contacted both victims at the university.

Like the first letter, the suspect changes the victim's name and has chosen a name from the Bible. He calls victim two Mary M., short for Mary Magdalene, a prostitute in the Bible. In this analysis, I am not sure if he is calling victim two this because of her many lovers, because he is becoming increasingly agitated, because neither victim has noticed him, or because he has an obsession with the culture of pimps and prostitutes. In both letters, the suspect uses the word *luv* as opposed to *love.* The words have two different meanings. "I luv you" in some circles is not as personal as the formal phrase "I love you."

CRIME SCENE BEHAVIOR

At this crime scene, the suspect had similar behaviors, yet they were much more aggressive. The suspect gained entry by burglarizing the front door of the residence using a hanger that can be obtained at any cleaners. The door is loose, and the lock is a key-in-the-knob lock, which was easily manipulated. Once in the house, the suspect entered victim two's bedroom, went through her dresser drawers to find the underwear and T-shirt drawers, and removed one pair of panties and one T-shirt. The suspect laid in victim two's bed and fantasized about having sex with her. However, he went a step further; the T-shirt was cut from the bottom up in the front center. There was a slit on each side at nipple height, and each of the cuts was covered in blood. In addition, the panties were blood stained and contained semen. The suspect masturbated using victim two's panties. This act is supported by the evidence and in the following statement: "I left you these panties they have something in tem, I like to call it my pimp juice. Wear them when you sleep at night then I will be with you at night my pimp juice placed against my woman, and don't forget that." The suspect called the semen "pimp juice." The suspect also left bloody fingerprints on the letter, the bathroom sink, and bathroom window for no apparent reason.

OFFENDER CHARACTERISTICS

The suspect is very comfortable in his ability to commit these acts as well as confident that he will never be caught. It is clear that he is escalating based on the nature of the communication, the blood left at the crime scene, and that he masturbated in victim two's panties. We also have one bit of evidence that we did not have before; the suspect is a white male based on the DNA.

Since the suspect has been ignored by both victims, it is believed that he will strike gain. It is safe to say that this next victim will be someone that he can attack and control. The ultimate objective here is to consummate the act and have someone be his sex slave. Understand the suspect is not capable of having a rational relationship where there is give and take and sharing, so he must control his victim. This is corroborated if you examine his statements and how he signed letter number two, "The Mac," which if spelled correctly, "the Mack," is the street name for a pimp. Naming victim two Mary Magdalene, who was a prostitute in the Bible; the use of the term *luv* instead of *love*; and describing his semen as "pimp juice" would leave one to believe that the suspect is fascinated with pimps and the control that they have over their women.

After the analysis of letter number two, it is my belief that the suspect will attack another victim. It is also believed that the suspect has already chosen this victim and that she is a student at the local college who is in the criminal justice program. The selection of victim two is something that is baffling because the suspect changed victim body types between victim one and victim two. Yet, historically, it is not the victim change that is important but the offender's signature, and in this case, it is laying out the victim's T-shirt and panties. However, based on the first letter, it is believed that a victim who fits the physical description of victim two is the most probable because of the suspect's description.

The age of the suspect can vary from early twenties to late fifties. The only clues to the suspect's age can be found in two conflicting details: the first is the use of the term *pimp juice,* which comes from a rap song by rapper Nelly, entitled *Pimp Juice,* released in 2002. The second is the suspect's chosen name, the Mack. *The Mack* is a movie about a pimp's rise and fall, which dates back to 1973. This suspect has crossed generational boundaries, and because of this, I am unable to successfully offer an age range. In addition, students attending the university and who are in the criminal justice program range in age from 18 to 70. And the professors range in age from 35 to 75. It is believed that the suspect is a member of this group because it appears to be someone who has contact with both victims at the university; however, it is someone who has gone unnoticed over time. What we do know is that the suspect is a white male.

Finally, there was an issue with the suspect's educational level based on the misspelled words. However, if you examine letter two, you will see that the suspect spells *shower* correctly, whereas he misspelled it in letter number one. In addition, the offender is believed to be a college student or professor. It is my belief that the suspect is using the misspelled words as a ploy in an attempt to throw investigators off track.

Index

About the Author

David J. Thomas, PhD, currently serves as an associate professor in the College of Professional Studies at Florida Gulf Coast University where he teaches in the Forensic Sciences Behavioral Analysis Program. He holds a doctorate in forensic psychology and a master's degree in education. His research interests include police, police/forensic psychology, serial homicide, victimology, violence, and terrorism.

Thomas served as a police officer in both Michigan and Florida, retiring from the Gainesville Police Department after 20 years of service. During his tenure as an officer, he held assignments in patrol, DUI enforcement, detectives, narcotics, training, community-oriented police team, and hostage negotiation and served as a field-training officer. Training is his specialty; he has been certified to train police recruits and in-service officers for the past 29 years. He is a certified expert in the Florida courts on the use of force. In addition to his academic duties, Thomas donates his time to the local police academy, mentoring and training new officers.